W9-APX-640

Pennsylvania

PENNSYLVANIA BY ROAD

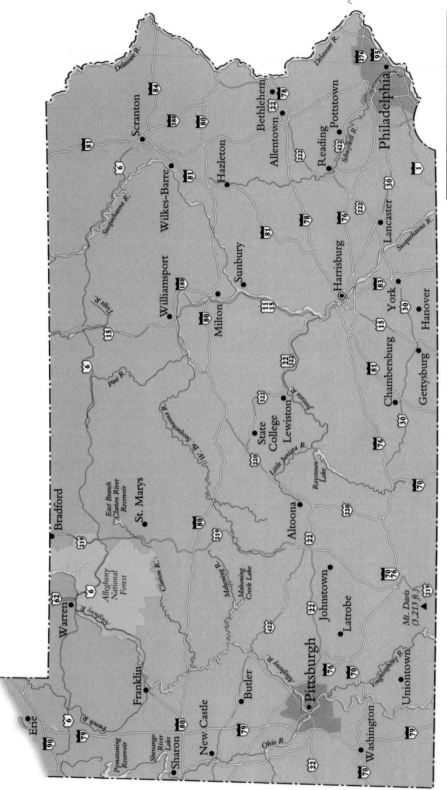

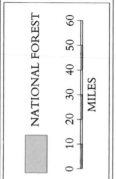

NATIONAL FOREST

MILES

0 10 20 30 40 50 60

Scranton
Bethlehem
Allentown
Reading
Pottstown
Philadelphia
Hazleton
Wilkes-Barre
Lancaster
Williamsport
Sunbury
Harrisburg
York
Hanover
Milton
Chambersburg
Gettysburg
State College
Lewiston
Altoona
St. Marys
Bradford
Johnstown
Latrobe
Warren
Franklin
Pittsburgh
Butler
New Castle
Sharon
Washington
Uniontown
Erie

Delaware R.
Schuylkill R.
Susquehanna R.
Tioga R.
Pine R.
Clarion R.
West Branch Susquehanna R.
Little Juniata R.
Juniata R.
Raystown Lake
East Branch Clarion River Reservoir
Mahoning R.
Mahoning Creek Lake
Allegheny National Forest
Allegheny R.
Youghiogheny R.
Ohio R.
French R.
Pymatuning Reservoir
Shenango River Lake

Mt. Davis (3,213 ft.)

N E S W

Celebrate the States

Pennsylvania

Stephen Peters and Joyce Hart

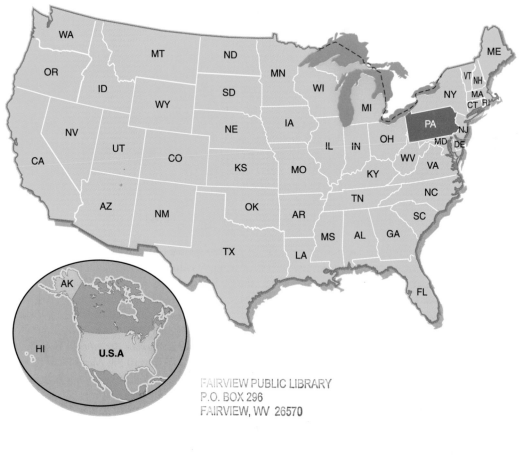

Marshall Cavendish
Benchmark
New York

Marshall Cavendish Benchmark
99 White Plains Road
Tarrytown, NY 10591-5502
www.marshallcavendish.us

All Internet addresses were correct and accurate at the time of printing.
Library of Congress Cataloging-in-Publication Data
Peters, Stephen.
Pennsylvania / by Stephen Peters and Joyce Hart. — 2nd ed.
p. cm. — (Celebrate the states)
Summary: "Provides comprehensive information on the geography, history, wildlife, governmental
structure, economy, cultural diversity, peoples, religion, and landmarks of
Pennsylvania"—Provided by publisher.
Includes bibliographical references and index.
ISBN 978-0-7614-3403-0
1. Pennsylvania—Juvenile literature. I. Hart, Joyce, 1954– II. Title.
F149.3.P48 2009
974.8—dc22
2008008032

Editor: Christine Florie
Publisher: Michelle Bisson
Art Director: Anahid Hamparian
Series Designer: Adam Mietlowski

Photo research by Connie Gardner

Cover photo by Ron Bennett/Digital Railroad

The photographs in this book are used by permission and through the courtesy of: *SuperStock:* Richard
Cummins, back cover; age footstock, 16, 103(T); Michael Gadomski, 58, 86; *Dembinsky Photo
Associates:* Michael Gadomski, 8; Skip Moody, 18; Alan G. Nelson, 107; *age footstock:* SuperStock, 11;
Danita Delimont: Jon Arnold, 12; *Corbis:* Bob Krist, 14, 72, 78, 79, 115, 134; Bettmann, 37, 47, 117,
125; Peter Turnley, 57; Rob Howard, 59; Hans Schmied, 111; Jason Cohn, 113; CORBIS, 123; Richard
T. Nowitz, 137; *Mark Gibson:* 82, 96, 132; *Digital Railroad:* Phil Degginger, 48; Conrad Gloos, 50; Ron
Bennett, 54; Richard Shaffer, 97; *Granger Collection:* 24, 26, 34, 44; *Bridgeman Art Library:* Baron von
Steuben drilling American recruits at Valley Forge in 1778. 1911(oil on canvas) 38; *North Wind Picture
Archive:* 28, 29, 30, 31, 33, 40; *Getty Images:* Hulton Archive, 42, 119; David Joel, 76; Ross M.
Horwitz, 17; William Thomas Cain, 85; Sylvan Grandadam, 98; CBS Photo Archive, 121; Gabriel
Bouys, 127; *The Image Works:* Mark Ludak, 52, 70; David Wells, 62; Joe Sohm, 64; Andre Jenny, 84;
Topham, 130; *Alamy:* Jim West, 71; Larry Lefever, 74; Classic Stock, 89; *AP Photo:* AMNH, 19;
Carolyn Kaster, 66, 100; Gene J. Puskar, 87; *Minden Pictures:* Jim Brandenburg, 21; Tim Fitzharris, 22;
Art Life Images: Blair Seitz, 91, Kord.com, 103(B).

Printed in Malaysia
1 3 5 6 4 2

Contents

Pennsylvania Is . . .

Pennsylvania is a scenic place . . .

"Our road wound through the pleasant valley of the Susquehanna; the river, dotted with innumerable green islands, lay upon our right; on the left, a steep ascent, craggy with broken rock, and dark with pine trees. . . . The gloom of evening gave it all an air of mystery and silence which greatly enhanced its natural interest."

—Charles Dickens, writer

"Nowhere in this country, from sea to sea, does nature comfort us with such assurance of plenty, such rich and tranquil beauty as those unsung, unpainted hills of Pennsylvania."

—Rebecca Harding Davis, writer

. . . rich in natural resources.

"Pennsylvania coal is what made this country run!"

—Tom Rusin, coal miner

"I think our forests should be preserved as much as humanly possible for recreation and just for enjoyment of the natural beauty of Pennsylvania."

—Ed Rendell, governor, 2008

Pennsylvania is historic . . .

"I never liked history before I moved to this little town, but I do now. You've got early German settlers, the stagecoach line, and the Underground Railroad all right here."

—Sarah Gavazzi, restaurant owner

"[Pennsylvania] is the cradle of toleration and freedom of religion."

—President Thomas Jefferson

"I lived in Pennsylvania as a kid and loved roaming the woods and finding historical artifacts just lying on the ground around me. It brought history to life."

—Ken Shimkets, retired business owner

. . . it is inspirational . . .

"Throughout Pennsylvania's small towns, big cities, and farm villages, old-world customs and traditional folkways unite with a modern aesthetic to produce some of the most spectacular handcrafted goods you'll ever see."

—Pennsylvania Department of Community and Economic Development

. . . and it is a great place to call home.

"Pennsylvania? I think of the rolling hills, the countryside, and meadows and streams . . . factories that made us what we are . . . the strong work ethic and sense of family."

—Jim Boyce, teacher

Pennsylvania is a place of pristine mountainsides and fertile valleys, of winding rivers and thick forests. It is a place of history and industry, of new beginnings for masses of immigrants anxious for a new way of life. Many people who are born here spend their lives close to the towns and the people they have grown up with. Others come back after having seen something of the world. Yet others come to go to school or to wander the state's wilderness and decide to make Pennsylvania their home. This state is the birthplace of the country's independence. It is a place where you can walk through hundreds of years of U.S. history in the morning and then enjoy the best of the twenty-first century in the afternoon.

Chapter One

Rich Land, Natural Beauty

Pennsylvania's variety of natural landscapes has resulted from millions of years of dramatic changes in the earth's crust. Continents shifting and crashing into one another created the state's mountains and valleys. The uplifted land masses eroded from eons of rain and the flow of the state's many rivers. Underlying the surface of the land are rich deposits of natural resources. The state's abundance of natural resources has made Pennsylvania both an industrial heartland of the United States as well as a rewarding and invigorating place to call home.

UNDER THE GROUND

What lies under Pennsylvania's soil is as important to its history as what lies aboveground. Between 600 million and 270 million years ago, much of present-day Pennsylvania lay beneath an ocean. Materials from the land washed into the shallows of this ocean, while shells and the remains of

The Susquehanna River courses through the hills and valleys of picturesque Pennsylvania.

life-forms collected in deeper parts of the water. A combination of pressure from the water and the earth's internal heat turned this material into rock. Likewise, in other time periods of the ancient past, vast swamp forests covered much of the land. Over a process that lasted millions of years, heat and pressure turned the plant matter of these swamps into coal and oil, which would fuel much of Pennsylvania's industry.

RIDGES, VALLEYS, AND FARMS

The Appalachian Mountains, which run from Canada to Alabama as well as through present-day Pennsylvania, once stood almost as tall as the modern-day Himalayan Mountains in Asia, at an estimated 20,000 feet high. Over millions of years, rain, rivers, streams, and glaciers wore down these majestic mountains. The result is today's varied Appalachian landscape. Mount Davis, the highest peak in Pennsylvania's portion of the mountain range, is only 3,213 feet high.

Another major aspect of the state's landscape includes the Piedmont, which is home to some of the richest natural farmland in the world. The Piedmont is located in the southeastern part of the state, between the Delaware River and the first ridges of the Appalachians. Although the cities of Philadelphia, Reading, Bethlehem, and Allentown have developed there, the Piedmont is still the state's agricultural heartland. This area is also home to a religious group called the Amish people, many of whom live and farm without modern conveniences such as electricity and tractors. Amish horses and buggies can often be seen rolling along the roads in this region, past miles of wheat and cornfields as well as colorfully painted Amish barns.

West of the Piedmont lies the Ridge and Valley Region, an area of long valleys and ridges running like a backslash across the state. In this region are cities such as Scranton and Wilkes-Barre. Driving on winding roads over one

Some Amish have established farms in the Piedmont region of Pennsylvania.

of these ridges and then dropping down into another valley is sometimes like entering a new world. Some of the smaller valleys are home to industrial factories and their associated small towns, all nestled into the hills. Other valleys, such as Great Valley, are broader. There visitors can find several Amish farms, seemingly untouched by the passing century. In contrast, Stone Valley contains miles of unbroken forests and endless dirt roads. Hunters, fishers, and hikers enjoy the wilderness there. Over Tussey Mountain, away from Stone Valley, is Penns Valley, which lies in the very center of the state. A combination of fertile soil and wilderness areas is found there.

At the western edge of the Ridge and Valley Region is the 1,500-foot-high Allegheny Front. This escarpment— a long, steep slope of rock—serves as a border with the next region, which is the Allegheny Plateau. Hawks, falcons, eagles, and ospreys migrate along the Allegheny Front in the fall.

The Allegheny Plateau stretches across parts of New York, Ohio, Kentucky, and Tennessee as well as Pennsylvania. The plateau is a tableland that slopes off across western Pennsylvania. Much of it is cut and eroded by winding streams and rivers, causing the region's roads to twist and turn through the forests and factory towns like roller coasters. A popular area for outdoor activities, the Laurel Highlands in the south support many ski resorts. In the north, the vast, wild areas of the Allegheny National Forest offer miles of skiing and snowmobiling trails. Because much oil, gas, and coal lie under the plateau's surface, this area is the center of Pennsylvania's heavy industry. Pittsburgh is the major city located in this region.

Pittsburgh is located in the Allegheny Plateau region of the state.

LAND AND WATER

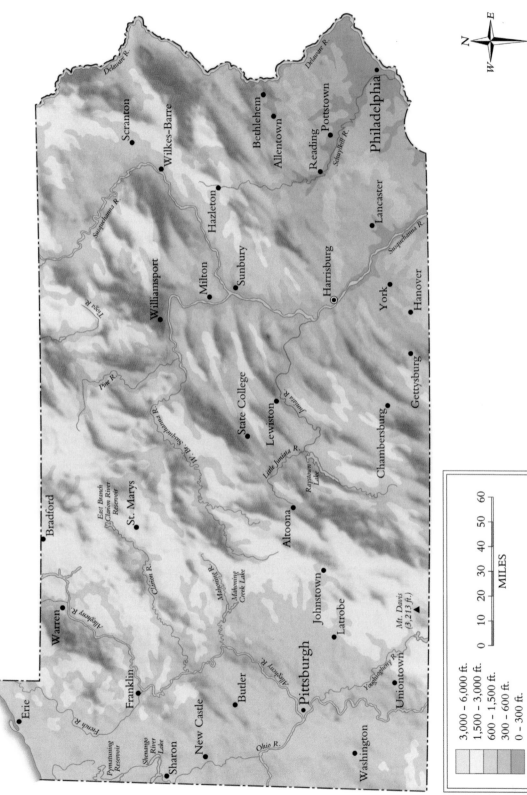

N
E
S
W

Scranton
Wilkes-Barre
Bethlehem
Allentown
Reading
Pottstown
Philadelphia
Delaware R.
Delaware R.
Schuylkill R.

Hazleton
Lancaster

Milton
Sunbury
Harrisburg
York
Hanover
Susquehanna R.
Susquehanna R.

Williamsport
Tioga R.

State College
Lewiston
Gettysburg
Chambersburg
Pine R.
Juniata R.
Little Juniata R.
Raystown Lake
W. Br. Susquehanna R.

Bradford
St. Marys
East Branch Clarion River Reservoir

Altoona

Warren
Allegheny R.
Johnstown
Latrobe
Mt. Davis
(3,213 ft.)
Clarion R.
Mahoning R.
Mahoning Creek Lake

Franklin
Butler
Pittsburgh
Uniontown
Loyalhanna R.
Allegheny R.
Youghiogheny R.

Erie
New Castle
Sharon
Washington
French R.
Pymatuning Reservoir
Shenango River Lake
Ohio R.

MILES						
0	10	20	30	40	50	60

3,000 – 6,000 ft.
1,500 – 3,000 ft.
600 – 1,500 ft.
300 – 600 ft.
0 – 300 ft.

Four great river systems—the Delaware, Susquehanna, Allegheny, and Ohio—shaped the region that would become Pennsylvania. They were especially important in the development of the state's transportation systems and industries.

The Delaware River defines most of the jagged eastern border of the state. It separates Pennsylvania from New York and New Jersey as it zigzags south through narrow rapids and wide, slow sections of the river from New York to the shipping ports of Delaware Bay at the Atlantic Ocean. Besides providing the major shipping lane in and out of Philadelphia, the Delaware River transverses major forested areas along Pennsylvania's eastern boundary. Large portions of the river are protected by the National Park Service.

Philadelphia is located on the shores of the Delaware River.

Along the northern border with New York is the 73-mile-long Upper Delaware Scenic and Recreational River. In the middle section of the river is the Delaware Water Gap National Recreation Area, a park that protects another 40 miles of this scenic river way.

Running north to south down the central section of the state, with east and west branches forming a treelike shape on the map, is the Susquehanna River. A favorite among tubers and white-water enthusiasts, the Susquehanna follows a meandering course through the mountains and ends its journey in the Atlantic Ocean at Chesapeake Bay. The Susquehanna River provides Harrisburg, the capital of Pennsylvania, with a major waterway.

In a similar north-to-south pattern, the Allegheny River flows down the western portion of the state, through the industrial city of Pittsburgh. Then the Allegheny joins the Ohio River and eventually flows into the Mississippi River to the Gulf of Mexico.

A SEASON FOR EVERYONE

Pennsylvanians enjoy four distinct seasons. Winter temperatures range from below zero to the fifties. Winter sports such as sledding, skiing, and snowmobiling are very popular. Although driving the icy mountain roads of central and northern Pennsylvania is sometimes difficult, the views are worth it. The snow-covered forests and countryside are so beautiful that they look like greeting cards. The lowest temperature recorded in Pennsylvania occurred on January 5, 1904, in Smethport. The thermometer fell to −42 degrees Fahrenheit.

Spring brings abundant rainfall and glorious blooms of yellow forsythia and redbud trees. Throughout spring, azaleas, rhododendrons, trilliums, jack-in-the-pulpits, dogwoods, elderberries, honeysuckles, black-eyed Susans, and mountain laurels bring splashes of color to the state's forests,

A field of wildflowers bloom in Hershey, Pennsylvania.

fields, and roadsides. In summer, the temperature rarely breaks 100 °F, but the humidity is often extremely high. How hot can it get in Pennsylvania? Well, on one of the more unusually hot days in Phoenixville on July 10, 1936, the temperature reached 111 °F. Pennsylvania's many cool rivers and lakes are great places to be in summer.

Maple trees blaze in red and gold during a Pennsylvania autumn.

Pennsylvanians seldom complain about the weather in the fall, when the leaves covering the mountain trees change color. "I went to college in Vermont, which is famous for its fall colors," said Katherine Maleney, who lives outside of Philadelphia, "but the first time I came home for fall break I could hardly believe my eyes. Everything was so beautiful. I love the way you get the goldenrod and the asters, not just the leaves. I love the way the plants and all the different trees blend in the fall. The other seasons are good here, too, but I like fall best."

FLORA AND FAUNA

Pennsylvania has a wide variety of plant and animal life. Nearly 60 percent of the state is covered in forest. Most of the state's trees are deciduous—meaning they lose their leaves—rather than evergreen. When the first Europeans arrived in America, the Pennsylvania area had many four-hundred-year-old trees. Though nearly all of this old growth is now gone, a few stands of virgin forest remain in the Allegheny National Forest and in Cook Forest State Park. Forests of maple, beech, and hemlock grow in abundance on the northern Allegheny Plateau. Ash, aspen, cherry, hickory, birch, oak, poplar, sycamore, and red and yellow maple do well in the southern parts of the state.

Animal life is varied, too. White-tailed deer, wild rabbits, black and gray squirrels, raccoons, beavers, foxes, mink, opossums, skunks, and woodchucks roam the state. Slightly less common, but still to be found around forest cabins and campsites, are black bears. Rarer still are wildcats, which live in some remote areas of the state. The Indiana bat, once common in Pennsylvania's more than one thousand caves, is now endangered.

White-tailed deer are a common sight in Pennsylvania.

THE BOG TURTLE: A THREATENED SPECIES

Bog turtles are so named because they live in bogs, swamps, and marshy meadows with slow-moving streams. They can be found in southeastern Pennsylvania. Bog turtles feed on a variety of plants and animals—insects, berries, and even the flesh of dead animals. When in danger, they burrow into the mucky bottoms of streams.

Development and selfish collectors have made the bog turtle an endangered species. As people drain wetlands for houses, shopping centers, and highways, these rare turtles lose the habitat necessary for their survival. Bog turtles also face pressure from reptile buffs who value them for their distinctive orange spots. At just 4 to 4.5 inches long, the bog turtle is one of the smallest turtles in North America. Reptile collectors find them cute—cute enough to make a great pet.

To prevent further loss of this rare species, state officials have persuaded many landowners to leave the bog turtles' habitat in its natural condition. Before the state begins a construction project, conservationists review the site to ensure that the turtles' habitat is protected. Also, the bog turtle has received federal threatened status, giving the species an extra layer of protection. To thwart illegal collection of the bog turtle, Pennsylvania gives a fine of $250 to $5,000 to anyone who is caught collecting this threatened species.

In addition, 373 species of birds have been seen in Pennsylvania. At night in the countryside, you often hear screech, great horned, and barn owls. In the woods are ruffed grouse, 2-foot-high wild turkeys, and the smaller bobwhite quail. Canada geese and mallard ducks are common on lakes and ponds. Great blue herons nest in the state's northwest corner, and songbirds are abundant in yards and meadows.

Pennsylvania also has many kinds of fish, reptiles, and amphibians. Bass, catfish, and sunfish are common. Many of the state's streams are excellent places to catch trout, and northern pike, walleye, bluegill, muskellunge, and black crappie can be found in lakes and reservoirs.

While most snakes in Pennsylvania are harmless, the state's reptile family includes three poisonous snake species: the copperhead, the timber rattlesnake, and the eastern Massasauga rattlesnake. The state is also home to wood, eastern box, and bog turtles. One of Pennsylvania's most important amphibian is the hellbender salamander. Environmentalists pay close attention to this 2-foot-long creature because it is extremely sensitive to pollution. Its presence is a sign of clean water.

Since the first European settlers came to Pennsylvania, the buffalo, native elk, moose, and timber wolf have been disappearing from the state. The state's list of extinct species includes twelve mammals, twenty-seven fish, six birds, two reptiles, and one amphibian. The greatest danger to Pennsylvania's remaining wildlife is the risk of habitat destruction by the building of parking lots, shopping malls, and houses. Since the 1950s, Pennsylvania has lost more than 4 million acres of farmland. When woodlands are cut down and fields are covered, the natural ecosystems are ruined. A growing number of Pennsylvanians believe that now is the time to act to prevent more loss of their natural world.

Ruffed grouse are just one of 373 bird species in Pennsylvania.

WADE ISLAND AND THE FIGHT FOR SURVIVAL

According to the Pennsylvania Game Commission, Wade Island, located in the Susquehanna River near Harrisburg, is a crucial area for black-crowned night heron (below) and the state's great egrets. Both birds are on Pennsylvania's endangered species list.

Scientists do not know why these birds have chosen Wade Island as their habitat, but state officials are trying to help the birds thrive there. There are more egret and heron nests on Wade Island than in any other place in Pennsylvania. There is a problem, however. The double-crested cormorant, a bird that is not threatened, is beginning to take over the island. Cormorants use the same type of nesting site as both egrets and herons. They also eat the same type of food, so the cormorant is becoming a threat to the two other birds. The cormorants were first spotted on Wade Island in 1996. Since then, their numbers have increased significantly faster than those of the egrets and the herons. The Pennsylvania Game Commission decided to take action.

The first plan was to place heron and egret decoys on a nearby island, in the hopes of luring the endangered birds to another location. This strategy proved unsuccessful. Commission staff also tried to discourage the cormorants by disturbing their nests. This did not work, either. The only action that proved successful was killing part of the cormorant population. Although this was a drastic move, it seemed like the only option. In the meantime, the Pennsylvania Game Commission hopes that its actions do not scare the egrets and herons away as well.

Although conservationists have reintroduced bald eagles, river otters, and Yellowstone elk into Pennsylvania's ecosystems, much work remains to be done. Jennifer Ottinger, a staff member at Hawk Mountain Sanctuary, says, "We need to have respect for all other beings in our world. That includes plant life and insects as well as other animals." Ottinger and many other Pennsylvanians have made conservation their life's work.

As Pennsylvanians gain a growing awareness and appreciation for the natural beauty of their state, they are working together to keep their homeland not just a great place to live but a healthy place, where all creatures have a chance to thrive.

Chapter Two

The Keystone State

On a map of the original thirteen American colonies, Pennsylvania is located right in the middle. The colony appears to hold the other colonies in place, much like the "keystone" that stonemasons put in the middle of an arch to hold the rest of the stones together. Because of this, Pennsylvania has been nicknamed the Keystone State, and in fact it has played many key roles in American history. In Pennsylvania, Americans declared independence, wrote the U.S. Constitution, set up a national capital, established a sound economy through heavy industry, and determined the course of the Civil War. They also nurtured American ideals of religious tolerance and brotherly love, values that formed a sound foundation for a growing nation.

NATIVE PENNSYLVANIANS

Ancient people, who appear to have come from present-day Eurasia, lived in the area that encompasses the modern state of Pennsylvania about 12,000 years ago. Note that this date is disputed by some scientists who think ancient people lived on this continent about 50,000 years ago.

This map of colonial America shows Pennsylvania's position among the original thirteen colonies.

Evidence indicates that the first people to live in this area, generally referred to as Paleo-Indians, eventually spread throughout present-day North America into several distinct groups. At first, these nomadic people hunted and gathered food as they traveled with the seasons.

More modern American Indians, living in the area of present-day Pennsylvania in the 1600s, included the Lenape (later called the Delaware by Europeans). The Lenape lived along the Delaware River, south of the Kittatinny Mountains, and on the Piedmont. In 1698 Pennsylvanian Gabriel Thomas wrote that the Lenape leaders were "slow and deliberate . . . naturally wise, and hardly to be out-witted."

Delaware Indians trade with European explorers in the area of present-day Pennsylvania.

They maintained their nutritional needs through hunting and gathering as well as through agriculture. The Lenape were a respected people among native tribes. They were sometimes called the Grandfather people because other tribes believed the Lenape had lived in the area the longest. The Lenape were some of the first people to make contact with European explorers.

Another native group was the Susquehannock, who lived along the Susquehanna River. A people with strong military and trading traditions, the Susquehannock surrounded their villages with stockades—tall fences that kept out wild animals and enemies. Inside these stockades, the Susquehannock lived in longhouses, buildings where several families lived side by side along a central passageway. Little is known about this tribe, as they tended to keep to themselves. When Europeans first encountered the Susquehannock in present-day Pennsylvania, a large village of maybe seven thousand was located near today's town of Lancaster.

A larger group called the Iroquois Nation, a confederacy of several tribes joined together, lived mostly in present-day New York, but they traveled to present-day Pennsylvania to hunt. The Iroquois had a strong economic philosophy that incorporated communal lands upon which they planted crops. They were also known for their skills in trading furs.

When the first Europeans set foot in Pennsylvania, about 15,000 American Indians most likely lived there. European settlers reported that the American Indians were generally tall; some historians speculate that American Indians had a better diet than Europeans at that time. These native people grew and ate corn, squash, and beans. Their diet also included potatoes, wild peas, maple syrup, wild plums and grapes, cranberries, strawberries, hickory nuts, chestnuts, and blackberries, as well as the meat of animals and wild fish.

SHARING THE WORKLOAD

Like many other native tribes, the Lenape guaranteed the success of their livelihood by sharing the workload. Woman and men had specific jobs, and their training began in childhood. Women were responsible for caring for the children, gathering wild foods, and planting and harvesting cultivated crops. Lenape women made clay pots and wove mats and baskets out of grasses. They also prepared the hides from the animals men caught by scraping off the hair, smoking the skin, and then cutting and sewing the pieces together to make clothing.

Typical jobs for Lenape men involved tilling the land for crops, making tools from stone, hunting animals, building canoes, and making weapons such as bows and arrows.

ARTIST: F. O. C. DARLEY.

In 1638 the first European settlers in present-day Pennsylvania carried the Swedish flag. They made a lasting contribution to the frontier by introducing the log cabin. Their small community near present-day Philadelphia, called New Sweden Colony, soon came under the control of Holland. The European powers were struggling over North America, and in 1664, not long after Holland took control of New Sweden, the Pennsylvania area fell under English rule.

Swedish settlers farm the new settlement of New Sweden Colony.

At about this time, King Charles II of England owed a large sum of money to Sir William Penn, who had recently died. This meant that Charles now owed the money to Sir William's son, also named William. The son, William, had recently converted to a new Protestant sect called the Religious Society of Friends. Outsiders tended to call these people Quakers because they were said to quake and tremble when they rose to speak during their religious services. The Quakers did not have ministers in the traditional sense. Instead, anyone who felt inspired could speak. Quakers did not believe in taking oaths or com-

William Penn created a settlement where people could practice religion freely.

mitting acts of violence. This meant that they refused to serve in armies. Many people persecuted the Quakers because of their beliefs.

The younger William Penn wanted to establish a haven where people like the Quakers could practice their religious beliefs freely. He asked that King Charles settle the debt to his father by giving him a large piece of land in the New World. This colony would be open to people of all faiths. Penn referred to the colony as his Holy Experiment. King Charles agreed. In 1681 the king granted Penn a large tract of land, which Penn wanted to name Sylvania, Latin for "woods." But the king insisted on honoring Penn's father by naming it Pennsylvania, "Penn's woods." In 1682 Penn and a group of Quakers sailed from England and established the city of Philadelphia, which means "City of Brotherly Love" in Greek.

William Penn and other colonists land at present-day Philadelphia.

CONTRADICTIONS IN PENN'S HOLY EXPERIMENT

Although Penn's Holy Experiment is associated with religious freedom, this tolerance had restrictions for certain groups. For example, Pennsylvania's original charter prevented non-Christians, such as Jews and Muslims, from voting or holding political office. Penn's definition of freedom also did not include enslaved Africans or African Americans. Penn himself was a slave owner.

Excluding the American-Indian population, Penn's colony grew from 500 people in 1682 to around 20,000 at the start of the 1700s. From the beginning, the Holy Experiment attracted a variety of people. In 1683 a large group of Germans settled just north of Philadelphia. Their leader, Francis Daniel Pastorius, wrote that "no one shall be disturbed on account of his belief, but freedom of conscience shall be granted to all inhabitants of the province."

Another religious group, the Moravians, moved into the Lehigh Valley in 1741. Like the Quakers, they had refused to conform to the state church at home. Other nonconforming groups included the Mennonites and the Amish, who settled the Susquehanna Valley and the rich farmland in Lancaster County. They and other German settlers came to be known as the Pennsylvania Dutch. This does not mean that they came from Holland. The word *Dutch* in this instance stands for *Deutsch*, the word for "German" in the German language.

In the 1700s many Presbyterian Scots-Irish people settled around present-day Harrisburg. In fact, around 1740, Irish migration was so popular that an Irishman wrote a song called "Off to Philadelphia." In 1773 alone, 162 ships from Ireland landed in Philadelphia.

Not all people came to Penn's Holy Experiment freely, however. The ship *Isabella* carried 150 slaves to Philadelphia in 1684. Though Quakers, Mennonites, and African Americans later worked together to abolish slavery, Quaker merchants of the time were as guilty as anyone of profiting from the slave trade.

While Penn treated the American Indians fairly, his successors did not. In the Walking Purchase of 1737, for example, the Lenape agreed to give away the amount of land a person could walk in one day. The colonists cheated by hiring professional athletes to run in relays, covering much more land than the Lenape thought they were giving away.

By 1750 Philadelphia had become the most important city in the British colonies. Despite its shortcomings, it was a forward-looking place with many firsts to its credit. The first written objection to slavery in the colonies was the Germantown Protest of 1688; Thomas Bond and Benjamin Franklin founded the first hospital in the colonies in 1751; and the Society for the Relief of Free Negroes Unlawfully Held in Bondage, the first organization working to end slavery in America, began in 1775.

By the mid-1700s, Philadelphia was a thriving city and the heart of the colonies.

SCIENTIST, AUTHOR, FOUNDING FATHER

In 1723 a teenaged Benjamin Franklin arrived in Philadelphia from Boston. He had little money at the time, but he would eventually become the city's most prominent citizen. A printer by trade, Franklin worked hard and bought a newspaper, the *Pennsylvania Gazette*, in 1729. A few years later he began publishing *Poor Richard's Almanack*, a book full of useful information and the witty sayings of "Poor Richard." The sayings included "Early to bed

and early to rise makes a man healthy, wealthy, and wise" and "Fish and visitors stink after three days." Franklin wrote these witticisms himself, though many people thought Poor Richard actually existed. Nearly every house in the colonies bought a copy of the *Almanack*. The book made Franklin famous.

Franklin also earned a reputation as a scientist. He experimented with electricity and invented bifocals, an efficient stove, and swimming fins. Though he only had two years of formal schooling, he was given the title Doctor, and he became the primary founder and shaper of what would become the University of Pennsylvania.

As a member of the Continental Congress, Franklin helped edit the Declaration of Independence, written by his friend Thomas Jefferson. Franklin also traveled to France to enlist French help during the American Revolution. Because the French loved *Poor Richard's Almanack*, they received Franklin warmly and helped him make many new friends for the American cause. At the end of the war, Franklin negotiated peace with the British and then returned home.

When he died at age eighty-four, Franklin was so loved and respected that 20,000 people attended his funeral.

FRONTIER VIOLENCE

As the colonies grew, the struggle to control the riches of North America continued. In the early 1700s, France controlled Canada and its lucrative fur trade. In the 1750s, to extend that trade, France began building forts along the southern shore of Lake Erie, in what was then English territory. Because of their religious beliefs, the Quaker-controlled government of the Pennsylvania colony refused to participate in military action to protect the British claims. As a result, the colony of Virginia sent troops under George Washington with a letter demanding that the French leave the British-controlled territory. The French commander refused, and, within a year, the French and Indian War (1754–1763) began.

The French were eventually driven out, but violence between the European settlers and the American Indians (who fought with the French in the war) continued. In one incident, a group of settlers from Paxton Township attacked a camp of peaceful Conestoga Indians in Lancaster County and killed six of them. When the survivors were taken to the Lancaster workhouse for protection, the Paxton Boys, as the attackers were called, struck again and murdered them. Many people in the colony supported the Paxton Boys. Other settlers were disgusted. Prominent Philadelphian Benjamin Franklin called the Paxton Boys "savages."

A NEW NATION

The French and Indian War was expensive, and to pay for it England levied heavy taxes on the American colonies. People in the colonies thought this was unfair because they had no representation in the British parliament. The cry "No taxation without representation!" became a popular protest.

In 1774 colonial leaders chose Philadelphia—then the largest city in the colonies—as the meeting place for the First Continental Congress.

THE ROBIN HOOD OF
CENTRAL PENNSYLVANIA: A LEGEND

When present-day Pennsylvania was still a frontier, a likable young man appeared. When he visited pioneer farms, he was polite, helped with the chores, and told funny stories. After he left, his hosts often found a pile of money with a note signed "David Lewis, the highwayman." Later he would become known as Davy or Robber Lewis.

Lewis was born in Carlisle in 1790. In the course of his illegal adventures, he was caught and jailed several times but always managed to escape before being taken to trial. People began to tell stories about this man who robbed from the rich and gave to the poor.

One story told of a posse searching through the mountains for him and meeting a cheerful fellow who said he'd actually seen David Lewis. He and the sheriff struck up such a pleasant conversation that the sheriff suggested that the fellow join them, which he did. The young man listened as the sheriff talked about his wife and children. After the posse got home, the sheriff received a letter signed "David Lewis, the highwayman." In it, Lewis thanked the sheriff for being such good company and wished good health to each member of the sheriff's family.

Lewis's escapades came to an end in 1820, after he was shot and captured. A few weeks later, he died in the Bellefonte jail of infection from his wound. What became of his money? Before his death, Lewis had written a letter to a friend, telling him that he could see where he'd hidden his treasure when he looked out his jailhouse window. Lewis's view was of the Indian Caverns. Since his death, many people have searched this area unsuccessfully for the lost treasure. Lewis was only thirty-years-old when he died. He is buried in Milesburg.

John Trumball's Declaration of Independence, 4 July, 1776, *is a celebrated painting that depicts the Second Continental Congress' approval of the Declaration of Independence.*

At this series of meetings, representatives would discuss their grievances with England. Two years later, on July 4, 1776, Philadelphia became the birthplace of the United States when the Second Continental Congress approved the Declaration of Independence.

England was determined to fight for the colonies, and in the late summer of 1777, British forces began marching toward Philadelphia. General George Washington, who led the newly formed Continental Army, was determined to stop the British at Brandywine Creek, west of Philadelphia. After the Battle of Germantown, however, the British occupied Philadelphia. Washington led his troops north to Valley Forge, where his men recuperated during the winter, and planned a new attack.

The winter provided little rest. Supplies were scarce. Even adequate boots were hard to come by. As a consequence, many soldiers had to resort to wrapping their feet in rags. Washington later wrote that "you might have tracked the army . . . by the blood of their feet." About 3,000 of Washington's 11,000 soldiers died of typhus, smallpox, and pneumonia during that winter. It seemed the army would surely fail at its next attempt to confront the British.

But Washington held his army together through that bitter cold of 1778, especially with the help of some Europeans. Prussian Baron Friedrich von Steuben and Frenchman Marquis de Lafayette, among others, helped to turn Washington's army into a disciplined fighting force. They also trained the troops in the latest battlefield strategies. Because of this help from the Europeans before and during the first battle after Valley Forge, the Continental Army shined.

During the harsh winter of 1778, Baron Friedrich von Steuben drilled recruits at Valley Forge.

PENNSYLVANIA BECOMES A STATE

The Revolutionary War ended in 1783. Representatives from the thirteen original colonies, now states, worked together in Philadelphia to create a constitution for their newly formed independent country, the United States. The colonists had won the war, but many challenges still lay before them. The new government established by the Continental Congress had little power. Even worse, the government lacked money.

Many Pennsylvania merchants and farmers, however, were not suffering. Some had profited from selling supplies to Washington's army. Others had made money by importing goods from Europe, a trade that increased significantly after the war. In 1790 a group of these wealthy businessmen came together to create the first Bank of the United States, which helped the government to stand a little more firmly on its young economic feet.

Problems still loomed. Revolutionary officials in Pennsylvania became wary of a centralized government. More moderate Pennsylvania leaders were in the majority, however, and they helped to ratify the first U.S. constitution. Pennsylvania's representatives were the second to ratify this document on December 12, 1787.

HARRISBURG NAMED PENNSYLVANIA'S CAPITAL

With the Susquehanna River running through it, the city of Harrisburg was an important trading center both for American Indians and later for the British. In 1719 John Harris established a ferry on the river, so early settlers first called the town Harris's Ferry. In 1812 Harrisburg was named the capital of Pennsylvania.

PROGRESS COMES WITH IMPROVED TRANSPORTATION

After the colonists won the Revolutionary War, Pennsylvania played an important role in the new nation. Philadelphia served as the nation's capital from 1790 until 1800, and the major route west to the expanding frontier ran through a huge gap in Pennsylvania's Appalachian Mountains. Settlers poured across Pennsylvania, and an atmosphere of progress and innovation blossomed. In 1794 the first major hard-surfaced road in the new country opened. It was the 70-mile-long Philadelphia–Lancaster Turnpike, which was paved with gravel and stone. Another aid to transportation during this time was Pennsylvania-born Robert Fulton's development of a practical and widely copied steamboat. Philadelphia's skilled shipbuilders provided the means for Pennsylvania's merchants to send their goods far beyond the state's borders.

In this energetic atmosphere, the "canal fever" of the early 1800s began. Mules pulled barges along a system of canals. The system cut the difficult Philadelphia-to-Pittsburgh trip from a month by wagon to five days by canal. One huge obstacle stood in the way of building a canal from east to west: the 1,500-foot Allegheny Front. An ingenious feat of engineering

Transporting goods from city to city became easier with the creation of Pennsylvania's canal system.

solved this problem. Crews loaded canal boats onto tracks. Then a steam-powered pulley system hauled the boats to the other side of the mountain, where they were put back into the water of the connecting canal.

THE CIVIL WAR

By 1860 tensions over slavery in the United States eventually led a group of Southern states to leave the Union. One year later they formed a separate country called the Confederate States of America. Newly elected president Abraham Lincoln stood firm against the breakup of the Union. The Civil War began on April 12, 1861. Pennsylvania played a key role.

About 340,000 Pennsylvanians served in the Civil War. Pennsylvania's highly developed iron industry supplied three-quarters of the Union army's cannons. The state's geography also helped decide the war. Confederate general Robert E. Lee wanted to invade the North and strike a blow to the Union's industrial heartland. He led his army up the Shenandoah Valley of Virginia into Pennsylvania. When a small contingent of his troops ran into part of the Union army, the Battle of Gettysburg began.

What began as a skirmish, the Battle of Gettysburg became the most important battle of the Civil War.

It would be the most decisive battle of the war. Beginning on July 1, 1863, the two armies fought in the field and woods outside Gettysburg. On the third day of fighting, Lee launched a desperate effort to break the Union's center. General George Pickett led between 12,000 and 15,000 men across open fields straight into massed Union troops. Pickett's Charge failed. By the time he retreated, more than half his men had been killed, captured, or wounded.

Tillie Pierce, a young girl living in Gettysburg, fled the town with her family on the battle's first day. Although they were seeking safety, they ended up very close to the fighting. Tillie and her sisters helped care for the wounded soldiers. "On this evening," she said of the second day, "the number of wounded brought to the place was indeed appalling. They were laid in different parts of the house. The orchard and space around the buildings were covered with the shattered and dying, and the barn became more and more crowded."

In all, 50,000 soldiers were either killed or wounded at Gettysburg. When General Lee retreated to Virginia, his line of hospital wagons stretched 17 miles. Though the war continued, the South had lost its last chance for victory.

The following November, the U.S. government established a national cemetery on the battlefield at Gettysburg. The organizers asked President Lincoln to say "a few appropriate words" at the dedication, though he was not the main speaker. His speech lasted only three minutes and received little applause, but the Gettysburg Address has since become one of the best-known speeches of all time.

LABOR AND INDUSTRY

After the war Pennsylvania continued to be a key industrial state, producing oil, iron, steel, coal, and other products. Andrew Carnegie built giant steel factories in Pittsburgh, where his workers did hard, hazardous work for little pay.

At the same time, coal increasingly fueled industries and heated homes. Waves of immigrants from Ireland and eastern and southern Europe poured in to work in Pennsylvania's booming coalfields and factories. This work presented unbelievable dangers. Men went into the mine shafts with open flames to light their way, and if they encountered gases, the chances of devastating explosions were great. Often mines caved in. Between 1870 and 1900 an estimated ten thousand Pennsylvania miners were killed at work. This does not include injured miners or those who died of black lung

Pennsylvania's coal miners work by the light of the flames on their hardhats.

disease from breathing coal dust. Like the steelworkers, the miners were paid little and had no financial security in case of injury. Though the steel and coal industries benefited the country, the workers paid a cruel price to keep the country running.

In 1892 workers at Carnegie's Homestead Steel Works went on strike when management announced changes in wages. Because Carnegie was in Europe at the time, Henry Clay Frick, his partner, handled the crisis. Frick refused to negotiate with the steelworkers' union. Instead, he brought in strikebreakers and an army of private detectives. The Battle of Homestead followed. For a whole day, workers fought the detectives and strikebreakers before the National Guard stopped them. Ten people died, many were wounded, and the strikers were forced back to work at lower wages. Not until much later did they form a union that could successfully bargain with management.

For the coal miners, progress came after John Mitchell organized the United Mine Workers Union (UMW). In 1902 UMW miners went on strike in the eastern Pennsylvania coalfields. The long strike continued into the winter. Many people around the country needed coal from eastern Pennsylvania to heat their homes, and supplies were low. President Theodore Roosevelt deemed this a national problem, so he stepped in and named a mediator. It was the first time presidential power had been used to settle a labor dispute.

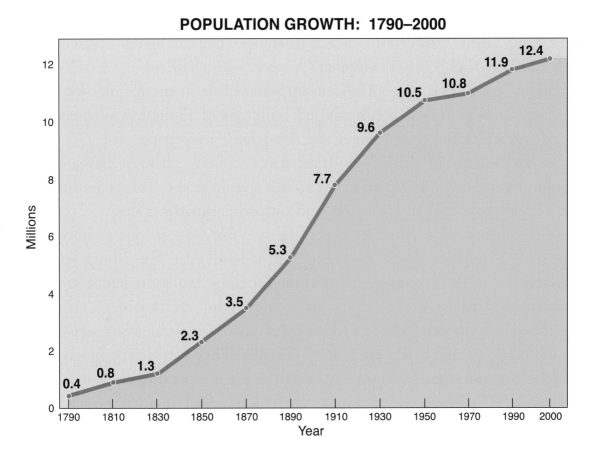

POPULATION GROWTH: 1790–2000

THE TWENTIETH CENTURY

When the United States entered World War I in 1917, the Philadelphia shipbuilding industry produced the warships. Thousands of men joined the armed forces, and the steel and coal industries supplied the industrial muscle needed to win.

Beginning in 1929, however, the Great Depression put more than one-third of Pennsylvania's workforce out of work. Whole families stood in long lines for hours just to get something to eat. "Even in bitter cold winter they waited," says Adelaide Haller, who lived through that time. "The bread lines stretched down the blocks and around the corner. Sometimes you couldn't even see where they ended."

The Great Depression ended when the United States entered World War II in 1941. Pennsylvania's steel mills, coalfields, and shipbuilding industries again played an important role in the nation's war effort. Pennsylvania also contributed hundreds of thousands of men and women to the armed forces and the defense industries.

After the end of World War II, the state's economy changed dramatically. Many steel mills closed in the 1970s, again putting workers on the unemployment rolls and bringing hard times to industrial towns.

Then, in a frightening moment, the nation's most serious nuclear power accident occurred at Three Mile Island near Harrisburg in March 1979. Because of a technical malfunction and some bad decisions, the plant's nuclear core overheated, and contaminated gas escaped into the atmosphere. On the third day of the accident, as many as 100,000 people began evacuating the area. They feared a complete meltdown and disaster. Eight days later the plant went into cold shutdown, the crisis ended, and most citizens returned to their homes. However, health problems in the area led many local residents to sue

A plant in Berwich, Pennsylvania, turns out military tanks in April 1941.

the company. Many people around the country instantly became anti-nuclear activists. Others, though, felt the accident led to more dependable safeguards in the nuclear power industry.

In 1971 radioactive gas escaped from the nuclear power plant on Three Mile Island.

TODAY

Pennsylvania is changing in a major way. For example, its rich farmland is slowly being paved over as cities and their suburbs continue to expand their boundaries. The number of Pennsylvania farms continues to drop sharply. In the past couple of decades, the number of dairy farms has dropped almost 60 percent. Farmlands and suburbia are bumping up against one another and causing friction. For example, suburban residents complain about the smell of farms, especially the fertilizer and manure.

The promise of jobs first caused people to move off the farms to the cities. Today, a declining U.S. economy has made jobs in Pennsylvania more difficult to find. In early 2008, Pennsylvania governor Edward G. Rendell stated that although unemployment in the state was lower than the national average—2007 ended with a record-breaking 5,817,800 jobs—he was still concerned about Pennsylvania's economic outlook.

Pennsylvanians, who once thrived on the production of steel and coal as well as agricultural products, know how to make transitions from one type of economy to another. The twenty-first century will undoubtedly bring about changes in the lives of the state's population. Service industries, such as insurance and health-care providers, as well as high-tech industries, will provide the jobs of the future as cities grow and farms are taken over by large corporations. A keener awareness of environmental issues, such as threatened species and global warming, is helping to protect and to improve the state's natural landscape.

But some things will never change. Pennsylvania is still home to the beautiful Allegheny Mountains and to cities that are laden with a remarkable history—places that Pennsylvanians and tourists alike will always enjoy visiting or calling home.

Chapter Three
A State of Friends

Pennsylvania has a wealth of resources, but one of the most valuable is its people. In Pennsylvania, you will encounter people with fascinating backgrounds and passions. Some focus their energy on remembering their heritage, others on improving their community, and still others on simply enjoying life.

ETHNIC DIVERSITY

Starting with the original settlement of Penn's Holy Experiment, Pennsylvania has had a diverse population. Today, if you ask some of the 12.5 million Pennsylvanians where their ancestors came from, you will get a great array of answers. The largest single ethnic group can be traced to Germany. The next largest group is the Irish, followed by Italian and English. African Americans number about one million, 90 percent of whom live in the Philadelphia area. Gathering mostly in the eastern part of the state are more than 300,000 Hispanics. The majority come from Puerto Rico. "They see opportunity here and that's why they come," says Judy Delgado.

Pennsylvania is a state of smiling faces and people who take pride in all their state has to offer.

Smaller eastern European communities—Poles and Ukrainians, for example—live in towns where heavy industry once thrived. Reverend Arthur Turfa says, "People are still very proud of their heritage here. We don't use the [Polish] language in the service anymore, except for when we sing a certain hymn at Christmas. But a number of the older people can still speak the language, and we keep the recipes alive at home and whenever we have church suppers. People always bring *holubky* [noodles and cabbage] and pierogis [stuffed dumplings]." Pride in Pennsylvania's ethnic diversity is alive and well.

Ethnic diversity ranges far and wide in Pennsylvania.

ETHNIC PENNSYLVANIA

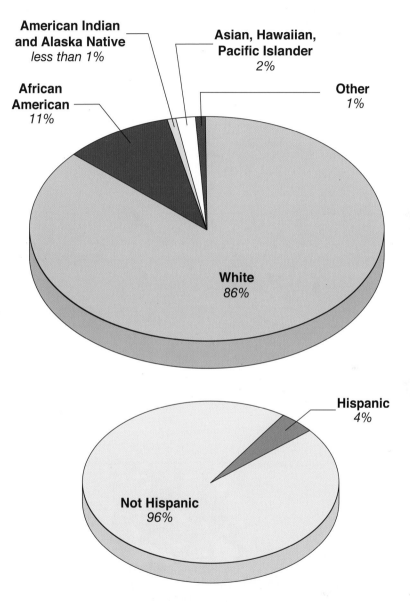

American Indian and Alaska Native
less than 1%

Asian, Hawaiian, Pacific Islander
2%

African American
11%

Other
1%

White
86%

Hispanic
4%

Not Hispanic
96%

Note: A person of Cuban, Mexican, Puerto Rican, South or Central American, or other Spanish culture or origin, regardless of race, is defined as Hispanic.

THE OLD ORDER AMISH

Imagine living without modern conveniences. No car, no television, no DVD player. You might not even have a telephone. Instead of going away to camp in summer, you stay home and work on the farm. You milk cows by hand. You weed the garden. You help cut hay in the fields and stack it in the barn. Or you help cook and serve food to the workers. There is always plenty of good food and plenty of hard work to do. For fun, you play in a creek or go with your parents to the barn, where cattle are bought and sold. You finish school after the eighth grade, and then you go to work on the farm.

That's what life might be like if you were born into the Amish community. The Amish are a deeply religious people who live on beautiful farms throughout Pennsylvania and the Midwest. Descended from a German-speaking Swiss religious group, Amish people do not believe in using modern conveniences because they feel closer to God if they live a simple, plain life. They have lived in much the same way since joining William Penn's Holy Experiment in the early 1700s.

COMMUNITY INVOLVEMENT

Eighty percent of Pennsylvanians who were born in the state still live there. This suggests that people care about where they live and have a real stake in it.

Pennsylvanians' deep commitment to their home state shows in a number of ways. The Quaker influence, which began with William Penn, is one. Philadelphian Thom Jeavons explains why Quakers traditionally engage in social action: "We struggle," he says, "to make our faith relevant and to give it expression."

An example of this involvement can be found in the Friends Workcamp Program, whose volunteers have helped improve Philadelphia's inner city since the 1930s. In a typical work camp, people live in the inner city and do home repairs alongside the home owners. A project may include painting, repairing damaged walls, or laying linoleum on a kitchen floor. While the campers work, they get to know about life in the city. The camp, as stated on the Web site, "offers an opportunity to increase awareness of economic, racial and cultural differences and inequalities as well as discover similarities."

Another organization, Concerned Black Men, was founded in Philadelphia but is now nationwide. It started with five African-American police officers who wanted to overcome some Philadelphians' negative stereotypes of young people. The officers wanted to highlight all the positive and creative contributions young people were making to their communities. Concerned Black Men encourages young people to be proud of their heritage, to take advantage of educational opportunities, and to live socially conscious lives.

In Philadelphia the organization offers scholarships, college tours, a program for adults to mentor boys and girls, a science program, and even a rowing team. All the adults are volunteers. Marq F. Temple, 2008 chairman of the Philadelphia chapter, says, "It is our universal bind of brotherly love that drives our commitment to serving our youth."

THE BRIDAL DANCE OF WESTERN PENNSYLVANIA

Some eastern European customs have been adapted into marriage celebrations in western Pennsylvania. One is the rollicking "bridal dance." In this custom, the wedding guests line up to dance with the bride. Each gets a brief turn with her. Those who have danced with the bride join hands and dance in a circle around her. Each new person joins this circle until all the guests are holding hands and dancing around the bride. At a large wedding, hundreds of people will surround the bride.

Then, at the most exciting moment, the groom enters the room and tries to break through the circle to get to his new wife. A group of his friends stops him and wrestles him to the floor. They then lift him over their heads, and he is carried hand-over-hand across the heads of the guests and is given to his bride. He picks her up and carries her off to their honeymoon as everyone cheers.

ENTHUSIASTIC ABOUT SPORTS

Watch the lines of cars driving through the mountains of central Pennsylvania on a weekend when Penn State's Nittany Lions play football. Then walk through the huge parking lots around Beaver Stadium and smell the barbecues of the tailgaters. You will see just two examples of how much Pennsylvanians love their sports teams.

Pennsylvanians enthusiastically support their professional teams, such as the National Football League's Eagles and Steelers, baseball's Phillies and Pirates, hockey's Flyers and Penguins, and basketball's 76ers.

Fans of the Easton High School Red Rovers football team cheer their team on.

Sometimes enthusiasm for sports leads to arguments, such as when people in Pittsburgh say theirs is a bigger sports town than Philadelphia. Pittsburghers like to remind the rest of the state that their Steelers have played in the Super Bowl six times and have won five of those games. They also boast that the Pittsburgh area has produced some of the country's greatest quarterbacks, including Jim Kelly, Joe Namath, Joe Montana, Dan Marino, and Johnny Unitas.

Some Pennsylvanians would rather participate in sports than watch them. On weekends and during vacations, Pennsylvanians can go white-water rafting, kayaking, or canoeing on rivers and streams. They can also enjoy a hike on one of the state's many trails. Some people enjoy spelunking—exploring caves—while others like to spend their free time on one of the state's hundreds of golf courses or many ski slopes.

Some Pennsylvanians like to take to the great outdoors.

SHOOFLY PIE

The Pennsylvania Dutch are famous for their delicious food. A favorite is the sweet and tasty shoofly pie. It probably got its name from the flies that loved its sweetness (and had to be shooed away) as much as people did. Everybody has a favorite family recipe. Have an adult help you with this one.

1 cup flour
2/3 cup brown sugar
1 tablespoon shortening
1 teaspoon baking soda
3/4 cup hot water
1 cup molasses
1 egg, beaten
1 9-inch unbaked pie shell

Combine the flour and brown sugar. Cut the shortening into the mixture until it gets crumbly. Set the mixture aside. Dissolve the baking soda into hot (but not boiling) water. Combine the molasses, egg, and baking soda water into a small bowl and beat the ingredients well. Pour this into the pie shell and sprinkle the flour and sugar mixture on top. Bake at 375 degrees for 35 minutes.

POPULATION DENSITY

Persons per square mile

| 160 to 299.9 | 300 to 2,999.9 | 3,000 to 66,940 |

| 0.0 to 0.9 | 1 to 6.9 | 7 to 79.9 | 80 to 159.9 |

PIKE

WAYNE

MONROE

NORTH-AMPTON

BUCKS

PHILADELPHIA

MONTGOMERY

DELAWARE

SUSQUEHANNA

LACKAWANNA

WYOMING

LUZERNE

CARBON

LEHIGH

BERKS

CHESTER

BRADFORD

SULLIVAN

COLUMBIA

SCHUYLKILL

LANCASTER

MONTOUR

NORTH-UMBERLAND

LEBANON

YORK

LYCOMING

UNION

SNYDER

DAUPHIN

TIOGA

CLINTON

PERRY

CUMBERLAND

ADAMS

JUNIATA

MIFFLIN

CENTRE

HUNTINGDON

FRANKLIN

FULTON

CAMERON

BLAIR

BEDFORD

MCKEAN

CLEARFIELD

ELK

CAMBRIA

JEFFERSON

INDIANA

SOMERSET

WARREN

FOREST

CLARION

ARMSTRONG

WESTMORELAND

VENANGO

BUTLER

ALLEGHENY

FAYETTE

ERIE

CRAWFORD

MERCER

LAWRENCE

BEAVER

WASHINGTON

GREENE

Ask people in the state to describe Pennsylvanians, and you will probably hear that they are friendly. Maybe this is one reason the state's tourist industry has grown so quickly. The slogan You Have a Friend in Pennsylvania used to appear on the state's license plates, and it still seems to apply.

Janine Heinser and her husband moved to Mansfield in northern Pennsylvania from Long Island, New York, where they grew up. "We came up here to visit," Janine says, "and we fell in love with it because everybody is so friendly and laid-back. We also thought it would be a good place to raise our kids."

RECENT IMMIGRANTS

Pennsylvania's recent immigrants have tended to settle around Philadelphia. For example, a thriving community of Palestinians lives in the northeastern corner of Philadelphia. This group of immigrants belongs to one extended family. They have come in waves mostly from Mukhmas, located in what is

PENNSYLVANIA'S BIG CITIES

Philadelphia, with an estimated population of just under 1.5 million (5 million in the metro area), is Pennsylvania's most populated city. It is the sixth most populated city in the United States. Pittsburgh, which has experienced a declining population in the past couple decades, ranks second in size, with a city population of about 312,000 and a metro population of about 2.3 million. Other large urban areas are Allentown, Erie, Reading, Scranton, Bethlehem, Lancaster, Harrisburg, and Altoona.

now called the West Bank (land occupied by Israel), between Jerusalem and Ramallah. They moved to Philadelphia to find jobs and a better way of life. They are a close-knit family whose members help one another face the challenges of business as well as day-to-day life. According to the Historical Society of Pennsylvania, most Palestinian immigration began with Radwan Aref, whose grandfather came to the United States in 1912. Since then, sisters and brothers, mothers and fathers, aunts, uncles, and cousins have all arrived in Pennsylvania to start their lives over.

Another group of immigrants in Philadelphia is Asian. These people come from countries such as India, Pakistan, Philippines, Cambodia, China, Korea, and Vietnam. According to the estimated 2006 U.S. Census, 39 percent of Philadelphia's immigrant population is from Asia, which makes it the largest group. Many of these people have come to the United States as professionals hired by large U.S. businesses and universities. Some have arrived as refugees from wars. These people have brought their diverse cultures and have added their distinct influences to the city. Restaurants, churches, and temples—and whole sections of town, such as Philadelphia's Chinatown (located in Center City)—offer all citizens new perspectives on life.

Another 24 percent of Philadelphia's immigrants comes from South and Central America, including people

Although Asians make up only 2 percent of Pennsylvania's population, their culture and heritage is evident through traditional celebrations.

from the Caribbean. These include both old and new waves of immigration. Philadelphia began trading with Cuba and other Caribbean nations about two hundred years ago. More newly arrived immigrants come from Mexico, the Dominican Republic, Puerto Rico, and South American countries such as Colombia and Peru.

A much smaller percentage of new immigrants comes from African countries such as Eritrea, Ethiopia, Liberia, Ghana, and Nigeria. Like other immigrants, these Africans often come to join other family members or friends and to seek economic improvement. Many have settled in the western part of Philadelphia.

THE LENAPE NATION

Although there are no federally recognized American-Indian reservations remaining in Pennsylvania, there are still many people of this heritage living in the state. According to the 2006 U.S. Census estimated count, the number is almost 22,000. One of the largest groups of American Indians in Pennsylvania is the Lenape, whose ancestors lived in the area long before white Europeans settlers arrived. Recently, the Lenape people, many of whom live in Sellersville, joined with environmentalists, educators, and other people to keep the Lenape culture alive by sharing special cultural events. One of these events is the Rising Nation River Journey, a three-week canoe trip down the Delaware River. This annual event invokes an awareness of the Lenape culture and its history in Pennsylvania.

Pennsylvania was created in the spirit of brotherhood, as a coming together of people from various walks of life. The idea that people of many backgrounds can live together and learn from one another is still alive in the state.

Chapter Four

The Commonwealth

Pennsylvania is a commonwealth. This means that it is a state founded for the common good of the people. It adopted its present constitution, the fifth in its history, in 1968.

The Pennsylvania Constitution begins with a declaration of rights much like the Bill of Rights in the U.S. Constitution. In 1971 lawmakers adopted an amendment prohibiting discrimination based on sex. The state then adopted the Natural Resources and the Public Estate amendment in 1972. This law states that "the people have a right to clean air, pure water, and to the preservation of the natural, scenic, historic, and esthetic values of the environment." The state constitution provides the rules by which the government runs the state.

INSIDE GOVERNMENT

The constitution details the structure and duties of the three branches of government: legislative, executive, and judicial.

Legislative

The legislative branch, known as the general assembly, has two bodies—the house of representatives and the senate. The 203 members of the house are

Pennsylvania's law-making body, the general assembly, convenes at the state capitol in Harrisburg.

On January 2, 2007, members of Pennsylvania's House of Representatives take the oath of office.

elected for two-year terms, while the 50 members of the senate are elected for four-year terms. The general assembly drafts bills, which become laws if they pass both bodies and are signed by the governor.

Executive

The governor, who is elected to a four-year term, heads the executive branch. The governor is responsible for reading all the bills passed by the general assembly and then either vetoing (rejecting) them or signing them into law. The governor has the right to veto an entire bill or to choose only certain parts to veto. Unless both bodies of the general assembly vote by a two-thirds majority to override the governor's veto, the bill will not become law.

Other executive officers include the lieutenant governor, attorney general, auditor general, and state treasurer. These officials are also chosen in statewide elections.

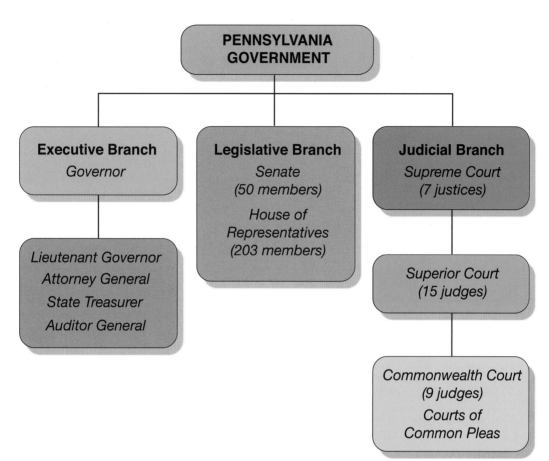

PENNSYLVANIA GOVERNMENT

Executive Branch
Governor

Lieutenant Governor
Attorney General
State Treasurer
Auditor General

Legislative Branch
Senate
(50 members)

House of
Representatives
(203 members)

Judicial Branch
Supreme Court
(7 justices)

Superior Court
(15 judges)

Commonwealth Court
(9 judges)
Courts of
Common Pleas

Judicial

The judicial branch interprets the laws by trying people accused of crimes and by settling disputes called civil cases. The supreme court is the highest court in the state. Seven justices sit on the supreme court, and each is elected to ten-year terms. They review cases on topics ranging from the death penalty to the constitutionality of established laws.

The superior court and the commonwealth court are statewide courts with judges who are elected to ten-year terms. The superior court hears civil and criminal appeals from the courts of common pleas in each county. The commonwealth court hears only civil cases that involve the state.

PENNSYLVANIA
BY COUNTY

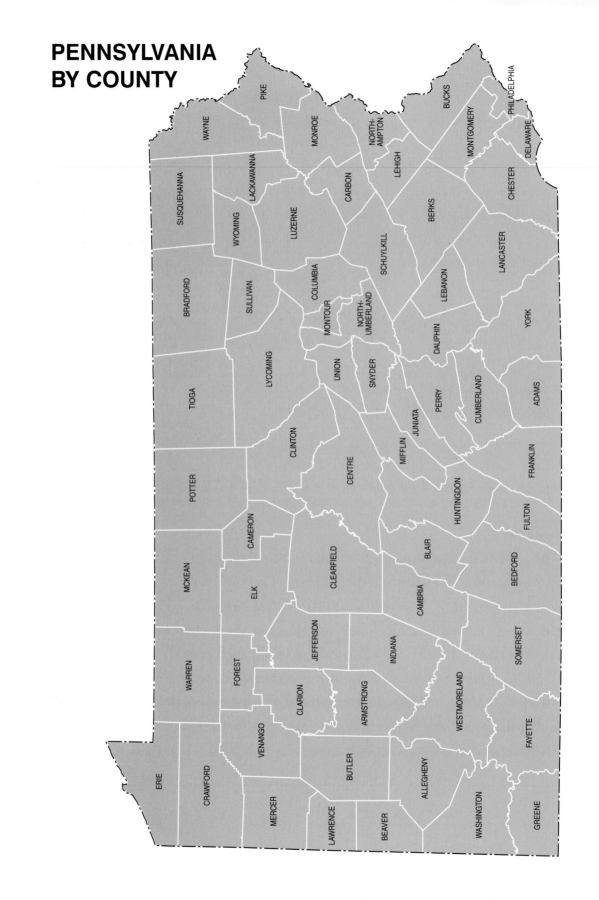

EDUCATION AND THE ENVIRONMENT

Education and the environment will dominate Pennsylvania politics in the twenty-first century. In a 2008 report named "Quality Counts," issued by *Education Week*, researchers found that Pennsylvania's public schools earned an above-average overall grade and Pennsylvania's educational system ranked in the top ten of all the states. None of the U.S. school systems earned a grade higher than a B, however. "We still have much work to do to ensure that every child graduates with the skills and knowledge needed to succeed beyond high school," says Pennsylvania's education secretary, Gerald L. Zahorchak. Zahorchak suggests the following strategies to raise the schools' grades even higher: adopt statewide graduation requirements to ensure that a high school diploma means a student is prepared to succeed in college or in the workforce; improve funding for early child education; require teacher preparation programs; and make sure that all schools have enough money to fully equip their classrooms. Without these implementations, Zahorchak says, Pennsylvania students will not be well prepared to further their education or to work in a field of their choice. This will put students at a disadvantage in today's global market. "We owe it to them," Zahorchak says, "and to the commonwealth, to make sure they emerge from high school ready to succeed."

Taking care of the environment will also remain an important issue for some time to come. Pennsylvania has made real progress in this area. For example, Pittsburgh, once known as the Smoky City because of the air pollution from its many factories, has improved its air quality. On an average of two days each summer, however, Pittsburgh still suffers from "red alert" days. On these days, according to the National Wildlife Federation, warnings must be issued because the air is not safe

Pennsylvania's educational system is ranked one of the best in the United States.

These wind turbines in Somerset generate 1,500 kilowatts of power. At full speed, the blades turn at 165 miles per hour.

to breathe. Like the rest of the state, Pittsburgh is suffering not only from local pollutants but also from the added effects of global warming. Pennsylvanians are working to combat these effects by switching to renewable energy sources, such as wind and the sun, and thus reducing pollutants in the air.

Pennsylvanians, working together with their government, strive to keep their schools and their environment in the best possible shape to serve future generations.

Chapter Five

Earning a Living

Pennsylvania has a diverse economy that is changing with the times. The three big sectors of Pennsylvania's economy are agriculture, manufacturing, and service industries.

AGRICULTURE

Even though the number of farms is decreasing, about 800,000 Pennsylvanians are employed in agriculture. They furnish products that range from beef and poultry to fruit and timber. Pennsylvania farmers raise the fourth largest number of dairy cows in the United States, and the state has the fifth largest milk production in the country. Pennsylvania poultry produces the third largest number of eggs in the nation. Raising turkeys and farming trout are also successful. Pennsylvania leads the nation in pounds of mushrooms grown; in 2006–2007, the state contributed more than 60 percent of the total U.S. production. Horse breeding is another important industry in the state.

Serving Philadelphia's famous cheesesteaks keeps this waiter busy.

Pennsylvania ranks third in the nation's production of eggs.

2006 GROSS STATE PRODUCT: $510 Million

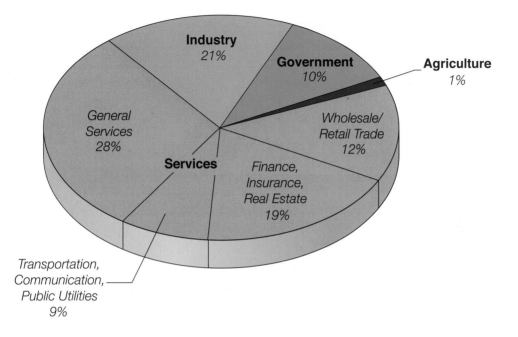

Industry
21%

Government
10%

Agriculture
1%

General Services 28%

Wholesale/ Retail Trade 12%

Services

Finance, Insurance, Real Estate 19%

Transportation, Communication, Public Utilities 9%

MANUFACTURING

Manufacturing and mining no longer play the central role in Pennsylvania, but they still account for about 25 percent of the state's economy. Manufacturing takes place mainly in Pittsburgh and in the eastern cities of Philadelphia, Bethlehem, Reading, and Allentown. Factories produce transportation equipment, electronics, printed materials, fabricated metals, industrial equipment, and food products. The state is first in the nation in production of snack foods such as potato chips, pretzels, and processed chocolate and cocoa. It is still a major producer of coal.

Pennsylvania's economy has been changing rapidly, but some areas have been left behind. This can be seen in the once-thriving mill and mining towns around the state. In the 1970s many of these factories and mines

Potato chips are quality control checked in Berwich, Pennsylvania.

PENNSYLVANIA WORKFORCE

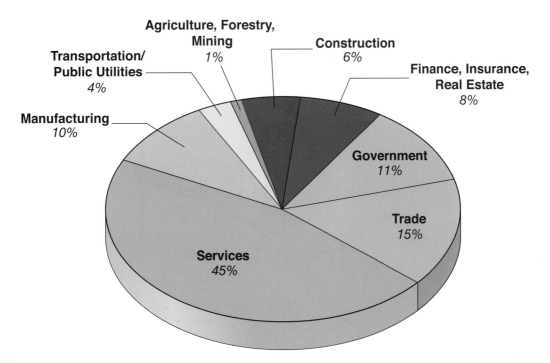

closed down. Now the towns are in transition, and leaders are looking for ways to breathe new economic life into them. Though the tourism industry has replaced many of the lost jobs, the problem is not likely to be solved completely soon.

SERVICE INDUSTRY

Pennsylvania's service industries are made up of many different types of jobs. One of the biggest is the government, which includes teachers in the school system and people who serve in the military. Other service jobs are found in insurance companies, hospitals and other health facilities, retail stores, and banks.

In recent years, another type of service job has grown faster than jobs in any other sector of Pennsylvania's economy. In 2007 tourism was ranked as the state's second largest industry. Jobs in the tourism industry include those found in restaurants, hotels, rental car businesses, and amusement parks and other tourist attractions.

A tour guide tells the history of the famous Liberty Bell in Philadelphia.

TOURIST AND RESIDENT BIKERS

Pennsylvania is a great state for biking. In 2006 *Bicycling Magazine* ranked the southern Alleghenies region one of the top five best bicycling areas in the country. This section of the state is home to the largest professional and amateur bike road race in the country, the annual Tour de Toona.

EARNING A LIVING

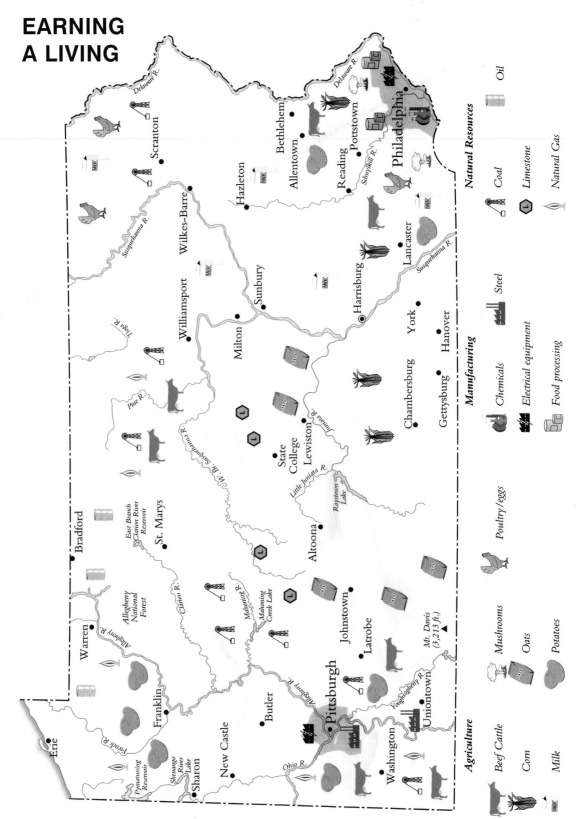

Natural Resources

Oil

Coal   Limestone

Natural Gas

Manufacturing

Steel

Chemicals   Electrical equipment

Food processing

Agriculture

Beef Cattle   Poultry/eggs   Mushrooms   Oats   Potatoes

Corn

Milk

The number of tourists visiting this state is increasing, and it is easy to see why so many people want to visit the state. Pennsylvania's many ski resorts attract visitors during the winter months, and major historical sites lure tourists all year long. Visitors can also enjoy excellent fishing, hiking, and camping. Many people visit the state on business, and the opportunity to watch major sports or to hear world-class orchestras in Philadelphia or Pittsburgh attracts others. Shoppers flock to the outlet stores of Reading, and vacationers enjoy family fun at amusement parks like Hersheypark near Harrisburg.

In 2007 many people's minds were on the economy, as the United States looked like it was headed for a recession (a significant decline in economic activity). This would, of course, affect Pennsylvania. But at the end of 2007, Pennsylvania's economy seemed to have the strength to face this challenge. With tourism on the rise and residents who seek to protect the state's natural beauty, Pennsylvania's economy seems headed toward a bright future.

Chapter Six

Pennsylvania's Sights

First-time visitors to Pennsylvania often think they already know what they are going to see. Some think they will see only cities and factories. Others think they will see only Amish farms and horses and buggies. They will see all of that, of course. But they will see much more, too. Pennsylvania offers the kinds of experiences people never forget. Let's take a quick drive through the state and find out more about what there is to see and do.

AROUND PHILADELPHIA

We'll begin where Pennsylvania began—in Philadelphia. The locals call it Philly. Independence National Historical Park is a good place to start. At Independence Hall, guides tell about the drafting of the Declaration of Independence and other historic events that took place there. At the Liberty Bell Pavilion, vistors learn that the Liberty Bell did not crack on July 4, 1776. Rather, the bell cracked the very first time it rang in 1752. Recast twice, the bell then cracked in 1835, when it rang for thirty-six hours after Chief Justice of the Supreme Court John Marshall died, and again in 1846, when it rang for George Washington's birthday.

Both Swann Fountain and City Hall are sites to see when visiting Philadelphia.

Another way to explore Philly is to visit the city's excellent museums. For example, if visitors are not able to visit the city on New Year's Day, when the uniquely Philadelphian Mummers hold their annual parade of string bands, fancy-dress brigades, grown men driving go-karts, and cavorting clowns, they can visit the Mummers' museum instead. On display are the crazy outfits that the Mummers, an organization of New Year's clubs that dates back to the 1840s, have worn through the years. Science buffs enjoy the Academy of Natural Sciences Museum, founded in 1812. One of its recent shows featured a fully animated dinosaur. If animals are a favorite, the Philadelphia Zoo, one of the oldest and best in the country, would be a great place to visit.

Mummers take to the streets of Philadelphia during their annual New Year's Day parade.

Hungry visitors can try the famous Philadelphia cheesesteak. One Philadelphian transplanted to Minnesota missed cheesesteaks so much that she actually had one of these steak, onion, and melted cheese sandwiches air-freighted across the country! "They always taste better when they are straight from Philly," she says. Trying a huge, hot Philly pretzel with lots of mustard or food shopping in the Italian neighborhood is always a treat.

North of Philly, at Valley Forge National Historical Park, is the house where George Washington spent his fateful winter during the Revolutionary

Made with steak, onions, and cheese, cheese, and more cheese—what's not to like about a Philadelphia cheesesteak sandwich?

War. Visitors see re-creations of the cabins his soldiers built. Farther north, in Bucks County, are some simple stone Quaker meetinghouses built in the 1680s. In New Hope there are mule-drawn barges on the Delaware Canal ready to take visitors for a ride.

POCONO MOUNTAIN REGION

Skiers can keep driving north to the Pocono Mountains, with their beautiful views and excellent ski slopes. Thirteen top-rated ski resorts and many state parks give outdoor enthusiasts plenty of options. At Ricketts Glen

State Park visitors can hike to twenty-two waterfalls, the highest of which is the 94-foot Ganoga Falls. Then there is the gorgeous Delaware Water Gap, where the Delaware River cuts through the mountains. This region is a favorite during fall, when the leaves turn spectacular colors.

If you're interested in history, Ashland is the place to be. At the Pioneer Tunnel Coal Mine, visitors can ride a narrow-gauge train 1,800 feet into a coal mine that closed in 1935. A guide explains how miners dug coal and hauled it to the surface with the help of mules.

Not far away is Hawk Mountain Sanctuary, a favorite of bird-watchers and hikers. Although the hiking trails are always spectacular, Hawk Mountain is an especially exciting place to be from September through November, when more than 20,000 raptors—birds of prey—fly over the area.

A hiker takes in the view of the Delaware Water Gap.

Driving west, tourists enter central Pennsylvania, an area of gentle beauty and wonderful surprises. Williamsport, along the Susquehanna River, is the birthplace of Little League baseball and the site of the annual Little League World Series. At the Little League Museum, visitors can see video highlights of past games and test their skills in the batting and pitching cages. Batters can see how well they did by watching video replays.

This little leaguer enjoys his homerun in the eighth inning of the Little League Championship game in Williamsport.

Farther west is Bellefonte, once a rich industrial town. The downtown, with its classic courthouse and square, evokes a slower time. Walking through this hilly town of restored mansions with turrets and fanciful, old-fashioned designs gives visitors an idea of what a wealthy nineteenth-century American town was like. Just down the road is the Mid State Trail, which follows Tussey Mountain overlooking Penns Valley. In Bald Eagle Valley, gliders soar quietly over the ridges on the same drafts of air that eagles ride.

TEN LARGEST CITIES

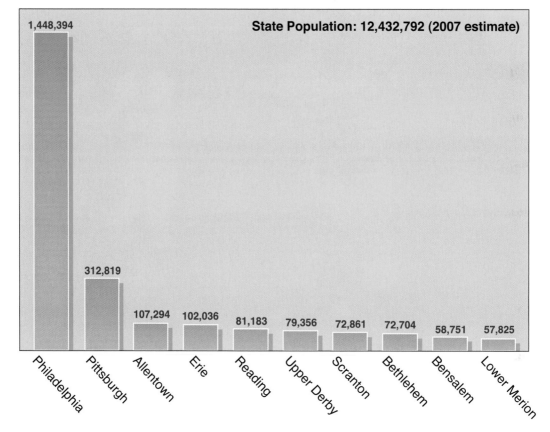

Driving north takes visitors far from city life. "We are so far removed from the rest of the state," says Tioga County historian Scott Gitchell, "it's hard to see how other things in the state affect us. Unless it's a really controversial issue, people up here don't pay a lot of attention. We're more interested in remembering our pioneer past."

Westward is the Grand Canyon of Pennsylvania, where visitors can stand next to the 50-mile-long, 1,000-foot-deep drop into Pine Creek Gorge. Some people enjoy rafting down the creek. Eugenia Keeney runs one of the many rafting rentals and teaches local history. "I was born and raised

This hiker admires the view of Pennsylvania's Grand Canyon.

here all my life," she says, grinning. "The King of the Canyon, Ed McCarthy, started doing this back in the 1950s with army surplus rafts. . . . He said his son and I lost our baby bottles floating down the creek. We grew up on the creek. I wouldn't live anywhere else."

Farther west is the Allegheny National Forest, Pennsylvania's only national forest. This is a great place for camping, hiking, biking, canoeing, or just driving scenic back roads. Many trails have been designated for cross-country skiing or snowmobiling. It is also the site of one of Pennsylvania's few old-growth forest stands, Tionesta Scenic Area, a truly magical place.

Nearby are the Drake Well Museum in Titusville and Oil Creek State Park, where visitors explore the early history of oil drilling. The park has 7,000 acres of trails that wind through ghost towns, cemeteries, and abandoned wells. The excursion train of the Oil Creek and Titusville Railroad is a fun way to see this area.

To the northwest are the shores of Lake Erie and Pennsylvania's third largest city, Erie. There, visitors can view a re-creation of the ship *Niagara*, commanded by Commodore Oliver Hazard Perry when he defeated the British fleet in the War of 1812. Erie is also the home of Waldameer Park and Water World, an amusement park featuring a host of thrilling rides and waterslides.

Beautiful beaches line Lake Erie. Hikers enjoy the natural scenery of Presque Isle State Park and the Erie National Wildlife Refuge.

PITTSBURGH

After driving south through the rolling countryside of western Pennsylvania, you will arrive in Pittsburgh, where big-city life reappears. Of the many sights in Pittsburgh, two are musts: the Carnegie Museum of Natural History and the Pittsburgh Zoo. At the natural history museum you can find gemstones, dinosaur skeletons, and exhibits of endangered plants and animals. Visitors can also ride an imaginary elevator deep into the earth to view the layers of rock underneath Pennsylvania's surface.

Towering dinosaur skeletons are on display at Pittsburgh's Carnegie Museum of Natural History.

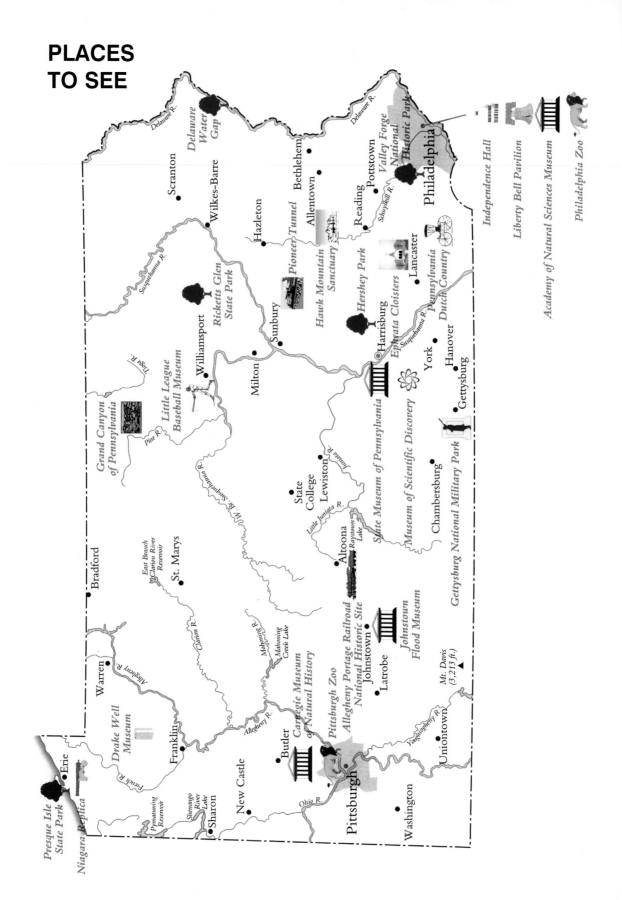

PLACES
TO SEE

Delaware R.

Delaware Water Gap

Delaware R.

Scranton

Wilkes-Barre

Bethlehem

Allentown

Pottstown

Valley Forge National Historic Park

Philadelphia

Independence Hall

Liberty Bell Pavilion

Academy of Natural Sciences Museum

Philadelphia Zoo

Hazleton

Pioneer Tunnel

Reading

Schuylkill R.

Susquehanna R.

Ricketts Glen State Park

Williamsport

Little League Baseball Museum

Sunbury

Milton

Hawk Mountain Sanctuary

Hershey Park

Lancaster

Pennsylvania Dutch Country

Harrisburg

Ephrata Cloisters

Susquehanna R.

York

Hanover

Gettysburg

Tioga R.

Grand Canyon of Pennsylvania

Pine R.

W. Br. Susquehanna R.

State College

Lewiston

Juniata R.

Little Juniata R.

State Museum of Pennsylvania

Museum of Scientific Discovery

Chambersburg

Gettysburg National Military Park

Bradford

East Branch Clarion River Reservoir

St. Marys

Clarion R.

Mahoning R.

Mahoning Creek Lake

Raystown Lake

Altoona

Allegheny Portage Railroad National Historic Site

Johnstown

Johnstown Flood Museum

Latrobe

Mt. Davis (3,213 ft.)

Warren

Allegheny R.

Drake Well Museum

Franklin

Carnegie Museum of Natural History

Pittsburgh Zoo

Uniontown

Youghiogheny R.

Presque Isle State Park

Niagara Replica

Erie

French Cr.

Pymatuning Reservoir

Shenango River Lake

Sharon

New Castle

Butler

Ohio R.

Pittsburgh

Washington

At the zoo, visitors can climb a giant rope spiderweb or experience life in the treetops at the Canopy Walk. Other exhibits take guests right into animal habitats under the ground or water.

THE SOUTHERN ALLEGHENIES

There is much to see of history, nature, and industry east of Pittsburgh. For history buffs, reenactors put on a good show of a French and Indian War battle at Fort Ligonier and a great depiction of early American life at Old Bedford Village. Some of the best skiing in the state can be found at Blue Knob Ski Resort. At Ohiopyle, the Youghiogheny (yock-a-GAY-nee) River cuts through the Laurel Ridge and creates a 1,700-foot-deep gorge that is popular with rafters.

Today, the southern Alleghenies' contribution to the industrial development of Pennsylvania is commemorated on the Path of Progress. Trails, parks, and heritage sites mark this 500-mile route. At the Allegheny Portage Railroad National Historic Site, atop Cresson Mountain, visitors can see models of the pulley system that carried people and canal boats across the Allegheny Front. Visit the 160-year-old Lemon House, the tavern where travelers stopped and ate during their crossing. Then go to see the Horseshoe Curve National Historic Landmark nearby. This curved track carries trains 85 feet higher each mile. Like the portage, it's an amazing feat of engineering.

Not to be missed along the Path of Progress is the Johnstown Flood Museum. In 1889 a neglected dam burst during a heavy rainfall. The 40-foot wave that crashed down the valley of the Little Conemaugh River picked up everything in its path. The wave smashed into Johnstown, killed more than two thousand people, and destroyed the town. The museum documents the flood with exhibits and an Academy Award–winning film.

THE JOHNSTOWN FLOOD

On May 31, 1889, the worst peacetime disaster in the nation's history took place when the South Fork Dam, 16 miles upstream from Johnstown, broke. It sent a roaring wall of water rushing down upon the city. When the waters subsided, a tremendous fire broke out, which added to the misery and destruction. The flood left 35,000 people homeless and 2,200 dead.

On a bal-my day in May, When na-ture held full sway, And the birds sang sweet-ly in the sky a-bove, A ci-ty lay se-rene in a val-ley deep and green, Where thou-sands dwelt in hap-pi-ness and love.

Chorus
Now, the cry of dis-tress from the east to the west, And our whole dear coun-try now is plunged in woe.

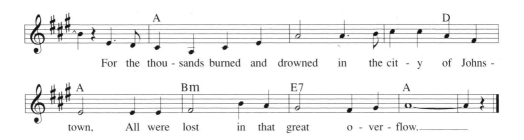

For the thou-sands burned and drowned in the cit - y of Johns - town, All were lost in that great o - ver - flow.

Like a Paul Revere of old,
Came a rider both brave and bold;
On a big bay horse he's flying like a deer.
Giving warning shrills,
"Quickly fly up to the hills."
But the people smiled and showed no signs of fear. *Chorus*

Ah! But e'er he turned away,
This brave rider and the bay,
And the many thousand souls he tried to save,
But they had no time to spare,
Nor to offer up a prayer.
Now they were swept off to a watery grave. *Chorus*

Fathers, mothers, children, all,
Both the young, old, great and small,
They were thrown about like chaff before the wind;
When the fearful raging flood,
Rushing where the city stood,
Leaving thousands dead and dying there behind. *Chorus*

Now the cry of fire arose,
Like the scream of battling foes,
For that dreadful sick'ning pile was now on fire.
As they poured out prayers to heaven,
They were burned as in an oven,
And that dreadful ruin formed their funeral pyre. *Chorus*

Driving east across the southern Alleghenies, we reach the beautifully pre-served Gettysburg Battlefield. Climb through the rocks of Little Round Top, the scene of fierce fighting. Walk across the open fields of Pickett's Charge. Local stables rent horses that take riders over large parts of the battlefield. Guides are also available to take visitors over the battlefield, and they tell stories that might otherwise never be learned.

Driving north from Gettysburg, we reach the state capital, Harrisburg. Like many of Pennsylvania's smaller cities, it's a pretty place with row houses and shaded streets. Spend time at the State Museum of Pennsylvania, which shows what Pennsylvania looked like 3.6 billion years ago. Then walk up the street to the Museum of Scientific Discovery, where interactive exhibits bring science to life.

Tourists view the battlefields of Gettysburg Military Park.

BRINGING THE CIVIL WAR TO LIFE

In the town of Gettysburg, during July, serious Civil War buffs reenact the Battle of Gettysburg. In 2008 the reenactment celebrated its 145th anniversary.

Jo An Yoder and her husband and son, who live in Lancaster, spend many of their free weekends taking part in Civil War reenactments. Her husband and son dress in Union artillery regiment uniforms, while Jo An dresses as a wife visiting from home. "The wives used to come to the camps and they would dress pretty to sort of cheer their husbands up," says Jo An. "Like today, I'm wearing the colors of the regiment in my dress. That's what some of the women would do."

Civil War reenactors work hard to make their clothing and equipment as faithful to the 1860s as possible. Jo An and her friends enjoy creating their costumes and uniforms. "I make hats and parasols for some of the other women. Then some of them make dresses or shawls or uniform shirts, and we trade. We help each other out." This is a way for Jo An and her family to socialize during their vacations. "We do reenactments all over and have developed a lot of friendships with other people who do this."

Driving east from Harrisburg, visitors enter the Dutch Country, one of the state's major tourist attractions. Here are miles of tidy Amish and Mennonite farms. Driving slowly on the back roads is a good idea because of the horses and buggies. It is also good to remember that the Amish are serious people living their lives according to their religious beliefs. It is impolite to take pictures of them without receiving permission.

Pennsylvania's Dutch Country is the home of the state's Amish and their farms.

CELEBRATING DUTCHINESS

Pennsylvanians of German ancestry take great pride in being Pennsylvania Dutch. After all, when many people think of Pennsylvania, they think of Amish farms, shoofly pie, and funny Dutchified sayings such as "The hurrier I go, the behinder I get."

For decades visitors have been dipping into Pennsylvania Dutch culture at the annual Kutztown Pennsylvania German Festival. It's a celebration of "Dutchiness" then and now. Craftspeople demonstrate quilt making, blacksmithing, weaving, and other skills. Expert marksmen demonstrate firing the Pennsylvania long rifle, which later became known as the Kentucky rifle. Old time Dutchy comedians entertain, polka bands play, and kids enjoy themselves at a hay maze and petting zoo.

"Komm rei, huck dich un essa!" say the posters for this get-together. ("Come in, sit down, and eat!") Indeed, that's the way it works. There is always plenty to do and plenty of delicious food to eat.

Another popular attraction is Hershey—chocolate-maker Milton Hershey's town. At Hershey's Chocolate World Visitor's Center, railcars take visitors on chocolate-making tours, and free samples are given out at the end. After that, visitors can head to the rides at Hersheypark or watch the animals at ZooAmerica. Indian Echo Caverns is nearby. There you can walk through rooms of magical rock formations with names like the Diamond Fairyland and hear about William Wilson, who lived in the caves for nineteen years.

Thrill seekers enjoy a day at Hersheypark.

Drive farther east to visit historic Ephrata Cloister, one of the more unusual communities in Penn's Holy Experiment. The members of the community believed that one grew closer to God by withdrawing from the world. Each brother and sister, as they were called, slept in a tiny cell, using a block of wood as a pillow. Strict vegetarians, they ate their first simple meal of the day at five o'clock. Great lovers of music, they composed more than a thousand hymns and chorales.

Today the brothers and sisters are all gone, but the historic buildings are well kept and worth touring. In 1777 General George Washington ordered that soldiers wounded at the Battle of Brandywine be taken there for care. One soldier later wrote, "I came upon these people by accident; I leave with regret."

In fact, that many people may feel regret at the end of touring Pennsylvania, where memories do last a lifetime.

THE FLAG: The state flag consists of the state coat of arms between two horses against a blue background. The coat of arms includes a ship, a plow, and wheat, which represent commerce and agriculture. Above is an eagle, symbolizing bravery. The olive branch below represents peace, and the cornstalk represents prosperity. The flag was adopted in 1907. The coat of arms includes the horses and motto.

THE SEAL: The state seal, which was adopted in 1791, includes a portion of the state coat of arms against a white background.

State Survey

Statehood: December 12, 1787

Origin of Name: *Pennsylvania* means "Penn's woods" in Latin. It was named in honor of Sir William Penn, the father of Pennsylvania's founder.

Nickname: Keystone State

Capital: Harrisburg

Motto: Virtue, Liberty, and Independence

Bird: ruffed grouse

Flower: mountain laurel

Tree: hemlock

Animal: white-tailed deer

Fish: brook trout

Insect: firefly

Ruffed grouse

Mountain laurel

PENNSYLVANIA

The official state song of the Commonwealth of Pennsylvania was adopted by the general assembly and signed into law by Governor Robert P. Casey on November 29, 1990.

Words and Music by
Eddie Khoury and Ronnie Bonner

GEOGRAPHY

Highest Point: 3,213 feet above sea level, at Mount Davis

Lowest Point: sea level, along the Delaware River

Area: 45,310 square miles

Greatest Distance North to South: 175 miles

Greatest Distance East to West: 306 miles

Bordering States: New York to the north, New Jersey to the east, Maryland and Delaware to the south, West Virginia to the south and west, Ohio to the west

Hottest Recorded Temperature: 111 ºF in Phoenixville on July 10, 1936

Coldest Recorded Temperature: −42 ºF in Smethport on January 5, 1904

Average Annual Precipitation: 41 inches

Major Rivers: Allegheny, Beaver, Conemaugh, Delaware, Juniata, Lehigh, Monongahela, Ohio, Schuylkill, Susquehanna, Youghiogheny

Major Lakes: Arthur, Conneaut, Erie, Pymatuning, Raystown

Trees: ash, aspen, basswood, beech, birch, black cherry, hemlock, hickory, maple, oak, pine, sycamore, walnut

Wild Plants: azalea, blackberry, bloodroot, bouncing bet, dogwood, fern, hepatica, honeysuckle, milkweed, raspberry, rhododendron, sundew, wintergreen

Animals: beaver, black bear, deer, mink, muskrat, rabbit, raccoon, squirrel, skunk, timber rattlesnake, turtle

Birds: barn swallow, bobwhite quail, Canada goose, duck, nuthatch, osprey, owl, partridge, pine grosbeak, ring-necked pheasant, wild turkey

Fish: Bass, brown trout, carp, catfish, chub, muskellunge, northern pike, pickerelm, walleye

Endangered Animals: black tern, short-eared owl, yellow-crowned night heron, black-crowned night heron, American bittern, common tern, least shrew, loggerhead shrike, Indiana bat, great egret, peregrine falcon, sedge wren, blackpoll warbler, Delmarva fox squirrel, yellow-bellied flycatcher, king rail, dwarf wedge mussel, ring pink, northern riffle-shell, eastern puma, piping plover, orange-foot pimple-back, rough pigtoe, cracking pearly-mussel, pink mucket, club-shell

Endangered Plants: northeastern bulrush

TIMELINE

Pennsylvania History

1500s The Lenni-Lenape, Erie, Nanticoke, Shawnee, and Susquehannock Indians live in present-day Pennsylvania.

Short-eared owl

1615 Dutch explorer Cornelius Hendricksen sails up the Delaware River to the site of present-day Philadelphia.

1638 New Sweden, the first European settlement in present-day Pennsylvania, is established near Philadelphia.

1643 The Dutch found Pennsylvania's first permanent European settlement on Tinicum Island.

1664 The English gain control of the Pennsylvania region.

1681 King Charles II of England grants Pennsylvania to William Penn.

1719 Pennsylvania's first newspaper, the *American Weekly Mercury*, begins publication in Philadelphia.

1754 The French and Indian War begins in western Pennsylvania.

1776 The Declaration of Independence is signed in Philadelphia.

1777 General George Washington and his troops settle in for a brutal winter at Valley Forge during the Revolutionary War.

1784 The *Pennsylvania Packet and General Advertiser* becomes the nation's first daily newspaper.

1787 The U.S. Constitution is drafted in Philadelphia; Pennsylvania becomes the second state to ratify the document.

1794 The country's first major hard-surfaced road opens between Philadelphia and Lancaster.

1797 Philadelphia carpenters walk off the job to demand a twelve-hour workday in the nation's first strike.

1812 Harrisburg becomes the state capital.

1825 The Schuylkill Canal opens, connecting Philadelphia and Reading.

1859 The nation's first commercially successful oil well is drilled near Titusville.

1861–1865 About 340,000 Pennsylvanians join the Union army during the Civil War.

1863 Union troops win the Battle of Gettysburg.

1889 More than two thousand people die in the Johnstown flood.

1892 Violence erupts during a strike at the Homestead steel plant.

1917 The United States enters World War I.

1920 KDKA in Pittsburgh, the nation's first commercial radio station, begins broadcasting.

1940 The first section of the Pennsylvania Turnpike opens.

1941 The United States enters World War II.

1971 The state legislature establishes an individual income tax and a state lottery.

1979 The worst nuclear accident in U.S. history occurs at the Three Mile Island power plant near Harrisburg.

1985 A group of tornadoes strikes parts of Pennsylvania and sixty-five people die.

2000 The Republican National Convention is held in Philadelphia.

2001 Passengers fight back against terrorists on United Airlines Flight 93. The plane crashes southeast of Pittsburgh.

2001 Tom Ridge, former governor of Pennsylvania, is appointed head of the newly established U.S. Department of Homeland Security.

2002 Nine coal miners are rescued after being trapped underground for seventy-seven hours in a mine near Somerset, Pennsylvania.

2005 The Philadelphia Eagles win the NFC football championship.

2006 The Pittsburgh Steelers win football's Super Bowl for the fifth time.

2008 Families of victims of Flight 93 (downed by terrorists on September 11, 2001) purchase the site of the crash, outside of Stoystown, to create a permanent memorial.

Agricultural Products: corn, hay, soy beans, mushrooms, apples, potatoes, winter wheat, oats, tobacco, grapes, peaches, chickens, cattle, sheep, pigs

Cattle

Manufactured Products: fabricated metal products, industrial machinery and equipment, transportation equipment, chemicals and pharmaceuticals, lumber and wood products, stone, clay, and glass products

Natural Resources: coal, iron, limestone, natural gas, oil, sand and gravel

Business and Trade: banking, health care, tourism, wholesale and retail trade

CALENDAR OF CELEBRATIONS

Mummer's Parade Philadelphia welcomes the New Year with its silliest parade, featuring banjo players, outrageous costumes, and go-karts.

Groundhog Day Each February 2, the eyes of the nation turn to the small town of Punxsutawney to witness the weather prediction made by a groundhog named Punxsutawney Phil. If he sees his shadow when he leaves his burrow, it means there will be six more weeks of winter. No shadow is a sign of an early spring.

National Ice-Carving Championship Competitors bring their blow-torches, chainsaws, and chisels to create wondrous sculptures at this February contest in Scranton.

Valborgsmassoafton Welcome spring in the traditional Swedish way at this joyous festival in Philadelphia. It features lots of singing, dancing, great food, and a spectacular bonfire.

Groundhog Day

Devon Horse Show and County Fair Each May in Devon, more than a thousand graceful horses compete in traditional events at the oldest outdoor multibreed equestrian show in the United States.

Kutztown Pennsylvania German Festival Everyone snacks on rich, delicious funnel cake at this celebration of Pennsylvania Dutch culture in Kutztown in late June and early July. Other favorites include pretzels, shoofly pie, and dumplings. Besides eating all the food, you can enjoy folk art displays, traditional music, and a reenactment of an Amish wedding.

Fourth of July Celebrate the birth of the nation in the city where the Declaration of Independence was signed. Each July, Philadelphia pulls out all the stops for more than a week's worth of parades, fireworks displays, concerts, sporting events, and as much food as you could possibly want.

Three Rivers Regatta Each July hundreds of boats take to the water where the Monongahela, Allegheny, and Ohio rivers meet in Pittsburgh. The event also features water shows and boat races.

HarborFest Harborcreek honors its place on Lake Erie each July with a festival that includes skydiving exhibitions, hot-air balloons, and lots of music.

Pennsylvania State Flaming Foliage Festival The tiny town of Renovo celebrates the brilliant colors of its trees each October with a parade, a crafts fair, and lots of leaf peeping.

Fourth of July

Bethlehem Christmas Guides in colonial costume take visitors on tours of Bethlehem's beautiful historic district during the Christmas season. You can also get into the holiday spirit with a candlelight concert or a ride in a horse-drawn carriage.

Washington Crossing the Delaware Each Christmas at Washington Crossing Historical Park in Bucks County, history buffs gather to reenact Washington and his troops crossing the Delaware River on their way to a decisive victory at the Revolutionary War's Battle of Trenton.

STATE STARS

Marian Anderson (1897–1993) possessed one of the greatest voices of the twentieth century. She began singing in church choirs as a young girl and eventually was trained as an opera singer. She first gained attention in 1925, when her prize for winning a singing competition was to perform with the New York Philharmonic. Anderson soon became highly regarded throughout Europe. In 1955 she became the first African American to sing at New York's Metropolitan Opera House. Anderson was born in Philadelphia.

Guion Bluford Jr. (1942–   ), an astronaut, was the first African American in space. Bluford was born in Philadelphia and attended Pennsylvania State University. He made the first of his four trips into space in 1983. He is now a retired U.S. Air Force colonel.

Nellie Bly (1864–1922) was a journalist famous for going undercover to expose corruption and abuse. She once spent ten days in a mental hospital to gather firsthand information about how the inmates

Marian Anderson

were treated. In 1890 she made worldwide headlines when she completed a round-the-world trip in less time than it had taken the character Phileas Fogg in the novel *Around the World in Eighty Days*. Bly made it in just seventy-two days. She was born Elizabeth Cochran Seaman in Cochran's Mill.

Ed Bradley (1941–2006), a prominent broadcast journalist, was born in Philadelphia and attended college in Cheyney. Bradley first gained attention as a reporter covering the Vietnam War for CBS. Eventually he was wounded by mortar fire. In 1976, when he began hosting the *CBS Sunday Night News*, he became the only black network anchor at the time. A few years later, Bradley became a featured reporter on the acclaimed television series *60 Minutes*. He won many awards, including several Emmys and the Overseas Press Club's Edward R. Murrow Award.

Alexander Calder (1898–1976), a sculptor born in Philadelphia, is best remembered for his whimsical mobiles. In the late 1920s he gained fame for making portraits out of wire. Later, his art became more abstract. Today, his large, graceful mobiles can be found in public buildings and museums around the world.

Andrew Carnegie (1835–1919) made a fortune in steel production and other industries. By the turn of the century, Carnegie controlled about one-quarter of American iron and steel production and was perhaps the richest man in the world. In 1901 Carnegie sold his company and retired. Today, Carnegie is remembered for his philanthropy. He donated $350 million to various causes and constructed 2,500 libraries around the world, along with many colleges and foundations. Carnegie was born in Scotland and moved to Allegheny as a child.

Andrew Carnegie

Rachel Carson (1907–1964), a marine biologist, was born in Springdale. Carson spent much of her career working for the U.S. Fish and Wildlife Service. She earned acclaim for her ability to write about science in elegant language in such books as *The Sea Around Us*, which won the National Book Award in 1952. Carson is best known for *Silent Spring*, which warned the nation about the danger of pesticides and led to the banning of a pesticide called DDT.

Mary Cassatt (1844–1926), a painter, was born in Allegheny and studied at the Pennsylvania Academy of the Fine Arts in Philadelphia. In 1866 she moved to France, where she fell in with the impressionists, who painted the effect of light on objects. In her paintings, Cassatt emphasized graceful lines and natural poses and often painted intimate scenes of mothers with their children. Her most famous works include *The Boating Party*, from 1893–1894, which hangs in the National Gallery in Washington, D.C.

Wilt Chamberlain (1936–1999), one of the greatest basketball players of all time, was born in Philadelphia. The 7-foot-1-inch center, known as Wilt the Stilt, was the leading scorer in the National Basketball Association (NBA) for seven straight years in the early 1960s and is the second all-time leading scorer in NBA history. His most phenomenal year was 1962, when he averaged fifty points per game for the entire season and scored a record one hundred points in one game. Chamberlain was elected to the Basketball Hall of Fame in 1978.

Bill Cosby (1937–), a popular actor and comedian, was born in Philadelphia. In the 1960s, when Cosby played a secret agent in *I Spy*, he became the first African American to star in a prime-time drama on television. His performances earned him the Best Actor Emmy for three years in a row. Cosby reached the peak of his popularity in the late 1980s on *The Cosby Show*, on which he played a warm and funny father of five. He has also written many popular books, including *Fatherhood* and *Time Flies*.

Bill Cosby

Stuart Davis (1894–1964) was an influential abstract painter. His most famous paintings incorporate bright colors and lively action, taking their inspiration from jazz music. Davis was also one of the first painters to use everyday objects such as billboards and street signs in his compositions. He was born in Philadelphia.

W. C. Fields (1879–1946), a comic actor from Philadelphia, was famous for creating grumpy, sharp-tongued characters who hate children, animals, and the police. Fields entered show business at age fourteen. Early on, he worked as a comic juggler. He eventually began performing on the New York stage and then starred in such films as *My Little Chickadee* and *Never Give a Sucker an Even Break*.

Benjamin Franklin (1706–1790), one of the most esteemed of all Americans, helped edit the Declaration of Independence and draft the U.S. Constitution. Franklin was born in Boston, Massachusetts. By age fiften he was writing articles for his brother's newspaper. In 1723 he moved to Philadelphia, where he founded the nation's first public library. He also bought the *Pennsylvania Gazette* and turned it into a witty and informative newspaper. Franklin later began publishing *Poor Richard's Almanack*, a wildly popular book full of advice. Franklin was also a scientist, famous for his electricity experiments and for inventing the Franklin stove. During and after the Revolutionary War, Franklin served as a diplomat in England and France, where his wit, intelligence, and integrity made him very popular.

Robert Fulton (1765–1815) of Lancaster County built the first efficient steamboat. One of Fulton's early designs was for a submarine, which he tried to sell to France. In 1807 his steamboat *Clermont* made a historic run from New York City to Albany, New York. This proved that steamships were trustworthy, and he received a patent for the invention. Fulton also designed the first steam-powered warship for the U.S. government.

Martha Graham (1894–1991) was the most influential figure in modern dance. As a dancer and choreographer, she favored stark staging and an expressive, dramatic style. Graham believed dance should use the body to convey true inner feelings. If the emotion being expressed was anger, jealousy, or fear, the movements might not be pretty. Graham's dances include *Appalachian Spring* and *Acrobats of God*. She was born in Allegheny.

Martha Graham

Milton Hershey (1857–1945) founded the company that became famous for Hershey's chocolate bars and Hershey's Kisses. He started his career as an apprentice candy maker in Lancaster. He eventually began making his own caramels and chocolate. Today, the company he founded remains one of the world's leading candy makers. Hershey was born in Derry Church, which was renamed Hershey after Milton established his business there.

Reggie Jackson (1946–   ) is baseball's sixth-leading home-run hitter of all time. Jackson spent most of his career with the Oakland A's and the New York Yankees. He led the Yankees to two World Series championships. Jackson's clutch play at the end of the season, particularly his four consecutive home runs in the 1977 World Series, earned him the nickname Mr. October. Jackson, who was elected to the National Baseball Hall of Fame in 1993, was born in Wyncote.

Gene Kelly (1912–1996) was an actor, dancer, and choreographer famous for his exuberant, athletic dancing in such films as *Singin' in the Rain* and *An American in Paris*. Kelly began dancing as a child, studying at his mother's dance school. He had already earned acclaim for his performance in *Pal Joey* on Broadway when he made his film debut in 1942 in *For Me and My Gal*. Kelly was born in Pittsburgh.

Grace Kelly (1929–1982), a Philadelphia native, was a well-known actress who became Princess Grace of Monaco. The elegant and sophisticated actress began her career on Broadway but soon began making films. She appeared in such classics as *High Noon*, *Rear Window*, and *Dial M for Murder* and earned an Academy Award for her

Grace Kelly

role in *The Country Girl*. In 1956 Kelly married Prince Rainier of Monaco. Although her career was soaring, she retired from acting.

George C. Marshall (1880–1959) was a soldier and diplomat born in Uniontown. Marshall was educated at the Virginia Military Institute. By 1939 he had risen to the rank of general and had been appointed the U.S. Army chief of staff. In 1947 Marshall became the U.S. Secretary of State. Perhaps his most lasting legacy was the Marshall Plan, a program of economic assistance to help rebuild war-torn Western Europe. Marshall's efforts in helping Europe recover from World War II earned him the 1953 Nobel Peace Prize.

Margaret Mead (1901–1978), a pioneering anthropologist best known for her studies of South Pacific cultures, was born in Philadelphia. In such books as *Coming of Age in Samoa*, Mead studied how children become part of their culture and how culture affects personality. For more than forty years, she was a curator at the American Museum of Natural History in New York.

Stan Musial (1920–   ) of Donora was one of the greatest baseball players in history. Musial played for the St. Louis Cardinals from 1941 to 1963 and later became the Cardinals' manager. An exceptionally smart and consistent hitter, he won the National League batting championship seven times and the Most Valuable Player Award three times. He also played in an amazing twenty-four All-Star Games. Musial was inducted into the National Baseball Hall of Fame in 1969.

Arnold Palmer (1929–   ), a Latrobe native, is a golf legend. Palmer was the first golfer to win the Masters Tournament four times and the first to win $1 million in prize money. His winning ways and charismatic, go-for-broke personality attracted legions of fans, who became known as Arnie's Army.

Robert E. Peary (1856–1920) is generally credited with being the first explorer to reach the North Pole. Peary began his career in the navy, in which he participated in surveys in Central America. His attention eventually turned northward, and he explored much of Greenland. Peary made several unsuccessful attempts to reach the North Pole before finally achieving his goal in 1909. Peary was born in Cresson.

Will Smith (1968–   ), a Philadelphia native, is a popular actor and rap singer. Smith began performing as a rap artist at age twelve. He soon began calling himself Fresh Prince, and he and his partner, DJ Jazzy Jeff, made several hit records while still in high school. With his amiable, engaging personality, Smith was soon starring in a television show called *The Fresh Prince of Bel Air*. Today, he is a leading film actor, having starred in such blockbusters as *Men in Black* and *Independence Day*.

Will Smith

Gertrude Stein (1874–1946) was a writer famous for her experimental style, which used simple language and very little punctuation. Her works include *Three Lives* and *The Autobiography of Alice B. Toklas*. Stein moved to Paris, France, in 1903 and lived there for the rest of her life. In Paris she was at the center of an intellectual circle that included novelist Ernest Hemingway and painters Pablo Picasso and Henri Matisse. Stein was an important early promoter of these and other modern artists and amassed an impressive collection of their work. She was born in Allegheny.

James Stewart (1908–1997), an actor from Indiana, Pennsylvania, was known for his honest characters and hesitant drawl. His many movies include *It's a Wonderful Life, Mr. Smith Goes to Washington*, and *Vertigo*. He earned an Academy Award in 1941 for his performance in *The Philadelphia Story*. In 1985 Stewart was awarded the Presidential Medal of Freedom, the U.S. government's highest civilian honor.

Ida M. Tarbell (1857–1944) was a journalist and a leading figure in the muckraking movement, which involved exposing corruption and abuse in business and politics. She is most famous for writing a book carefully documenting the business practices of the Standard Oil Company, which led to a government suit against the giant company. Tarbell also wrote a highly regarded biography of President Abraham Lincoln. She was born in Erie County.

John Updike (1932–   ) is a prominent novelist who writes about the dark side of suburban life. Among his many carefully crafted novels are *The Centaur*, which won the 1963 National Book Award, and *The Witches of Eastwick*. He is perhaps best known for a series of novels that follow a disillusioned man named Harry "Rabbit" Angstrom through the decades, including *Rabbit Is Rich* and *Rabbit at Rest*, both of which won Pulitzer Prizes. Updike was born in Reading.

Honus Wagner (1874–1955), who spent most of his career with the Pittsburgh Pirates, is considered the greatest shortstop in baseball history. He was both an excellent hitter and an amazing fielder. Swift and powerful, he was the National League batting champion eight times and the stolen base champion five times. He hit over .300 for seventeen years in a row, which is a National League record. In 1936 he became one of the first five players elected to the Baseball Hall of Fame. Wagner, nicknamed the Flying Dutchman because of his speed and Pennsylvania Dutch background, was born in Mansfield.

Andy Warhol (1928–1987), one of the most talked-about American artists of the twentieth century, was a leader in the pop art movement, which took its subjects from popular culture. He is best remembered for painting subjects such as Campbell's soup cans and the actress Marilyn Monroe. Warhol also made experimental motion pictures, including *Empire*, an eight-hour film of the Empire State Building in which nothing changes but the light. The Andy Warhol Museum, the largest museum in the United States devoted to a single artist, is in his hometown of Pittsburgh.

Andy Warhol

Daniel Hale Williams (1858–1931), an African-American physician from Hollidaysburg, performed the world's first successful open-heart surgery. Williams received his medical degree from Chicago Medical College, which is now part of Northwestern University. He later helped found Provident Hospital, the first hospital in Chicago to accept patients regardless of race and to hire blacks on staff. At Provident in 1893, Williams made medical history by repairing a heart suffering from a knife wound. Williams performed surgery at hospitals throughout Chicago and taught anatomy at Northwestern.

August Wilson (1945–2005) is a leading playwright whose work chronicles African-American life in the twentieth century. His plays, such as *Fences* and *The Piano Lesson* (both Pulitzer Prize winners), are noted for their humor, lively dialogue, and mixture of realism and fantasy. Wilson was born in Pittsburgh.

TOUR THE STATE

Gettysburg National Military Park (Gettysburg) Few people leave unmoved by a tour of the battlefield where more than 50,000 soldiers died. You can also visit the cemetery where President Abraham Lincoln made his famous address.

Hawk Mountain Sanctuary (Kempton) Although most people visit the sanctuary to see some of the thousands of birds of prey that pass through the region each autumn, it is also worth a stop for its wildflowers and hiking trails.

State Museum of Pennsylvania (Harrisburg) Ancient forests, ancient rocks, ancient peoples—you'll learn all about Pennsylvania's past at this fine museum.

State Museum

Rockville Bridge (Harrisburg) At 3,820 feet long, this span over the Susquehanna River is one of the world's largest stone arch bridges.

Hershey's Chocolate World (Hershey) There's no escaping chocolate in the town of Hershey—even the streetlights are shaped like Hershey's Kisses. A ride through Chocolate World will explain how the nation's favorite candy is made. At the end you get a free sample.

The People's Place (Intercourse) At this center dedicated to the Pennsylvania Dutch, you can attend school lessons given to Amish children, try your hand at the turn signals in an Amish carriage, and admire an extraordinary collection of quilts.

Valley Forge National Historical Park (King of Prussia) At this park you can imagine what it was like to have lived through a frigid winter during the Revolutionary War while also enjoying one of the most scenic parts of Pennsylvania.

Grand Carousel (Lahaska) You may want to hop on a carved tiger when you ride this beautiful 1922 carousel.

Independence National Historical Park (Philadelphia) Within just a few square blocks, you can see Independence Hall, where the Declaration of Independence was adopted; Carpenters' Hall, where the First Continental Congress met; the Liberty Bell; and Christ Church, which was attended by George Washington and other Founding Fathers.

Independence Hall

Philadelphia Zoo (Philadelphia) Look a lemur in the eye, roar with tigers, and pet a cuddly lamb at the oldest zoo in the United States.

Johnstown Flood Museum (Johnstown) This fascinating museum chronicles the disastrous flood of 1889, which destroyed the bustling city of Johnstown and killed more than two thousand people.

Fallingwater (Mill Run) One of the most famous buildings in the country, this house built over a waterfall is one of architect Frank Lloyd Wright's masterpieces.

Monongahela Incline (Pittsburgh) A trip on this trolley that climbs the side of a hill provides a spectacular view of Pittsburgh.

Peter J. McGovern Little League Museum (Williamsport) At this museum, you can take a swing in the batting cage and then watch your style on video. You can also watch highlights of past Little League World Series and learn about former Little Leaguers who made it big.

Pine Creek Gorge (Wellsboro) Known as the Grand Canyon of Pennsylvania, this majestic 1,100-foot-deep canyon is an ideal spot for boating, hiking, horseback riding, and skiing.

Niagara (Erie) This beautiful replica of the *Niagara*, Commodore Oliver Hazard Perry's flagship when he achieved his famous victory over the British during the War of 1812, was built in the 1980s.

Presque Isle State Park (Erie) A visit to Presque Isle might include relaxing on sandy beaches, spying migrating birds, or bicycling through lush forests. But no matter what you do, end your day watching the skies, for Presque Isle is an extraordinary place to watch sunsets over Lake Erie.

FUN FACTS

The Hershey plant in Hershey, Pennsylvania, is the world's largest chocolate factory.

Edwin Drake drilled the first successful oil well in the nation near Titusville in 1859.

Philadelphia has been the site of many firsts:

The colonies' first botanic garden was founded in Philadelphia by John Bartram in 1728. It is still in existence.

The first circulating library in the colonies was established in Philadelphia in 1731.

The first bank in the United States was the Bank of Pennsylvania (later renamed the Bank of North America), which began operating in Philadelphia in 1781.

In 1784 Philadelphia's *Pennsylvania Packet and General Advertiser* became America's first daily newspaper.

Hershey Chocolate Factory

Find Out More

To find out more about Pennsylvania, look for the following titles in your school or public library.

GENERAL STATE BOOKS

DeLeon, Clark. *Pennsylvania Curiosities: Quirky Characters, Roadside Oddities, and Other Offbeat Stuff*. Guilford, CT: Globe Pequot, 2004.

Huntington, Tom. *Pennsylvania Civil War Trails: The Guide to Battle Sites, Museums, and Towns*. Mechanicsburg, PA: Stackpole Books, 2007.

Mulligan, Steve, and Robert Hutchinson. *Wild and Scenic Pennsylvania*. San Francisco: Browntrout Publishers, 2004.

Richter, Daniel. *Native Americans' Pennsylvania*. University Park: Pennsylvania Historical Association, 2005.

Tassin, Susan Hutchison. *Pennsylvania Ghost Towns: Uncovering the Hidden Past*. Mechanicsburg, PA: Stackpole Books, 2007.

BOOKS ABOUT PEOPLE

Geiger, Charles. *Pennsylvania Landscapes and People*. Dubuque, IA: Kendall-Hunt, 2005.

Levine, Ellen. *Up Close: Rachel Carson*. New York: Puffin, 2008.

Mackall, Joe. *Plain Secrets: An Outsider among the Amish*. Boston: Beacon Press, 2007.

Moretta, John. *William Penn and the Quaker Legacy*. Essex, UK: Longman, 2006.

Stevick, Richard A. *Growing Up Amish: The Teenage Years*. Baltimore: Johns Hopkins University Press, 2007.

WEB SITES

To find out more about what is going on in Pennsylvania today, check out the following Internet sites.

The State Home Page

www.pa.gov/portal/server.pt

This site will give you loads of information about Pennsylvania and will connect you to links that explore special interests.

VisitPA

www.visitpa.com/visitpa/home.pa

Information about what to see and what is going on around Pennsylvania can be found at this Web site.

Pennsylvania's General Assembly Web Site

www.legis.state.pa.us/

Here you will find the name of your representative as well as what the state legislature is working on.

Pennsylvania Game Commission

www.pgc.state.pa.us/

On this Web site you will find information about the status of all major wildlife in Pennsylvania.

Pennsylvania State Parks

www.dcnr.state.pa.us/stateparks/

Want to go camping or on a long day hike? This site will tell you where the parks nearest to you are.

Roadside America

www.roadsideamerica.com/map/pa.html

From the best hamburger to the largest insect, this Web site provides fun places to visit along the highways in Pennsylvania.

Index

Page numbers in **boldface** are illustrations and charts.

ABOUT THE AUTHORS

Stephen Peters grew up in Pennsylvania. He went to elementary school in New Hope and lived in a house with the Delaware River at the end of his backyard. He later went to Milton Hershey School in Hershey, where he milked cows for Hershey's milk chocolate. He now works as a writer, teacher, and storyteller.

Joyce Hart's grandparents, immigrants from Italy, moved to Latrobe with their thirteen children. The men went to work in the Pennsylvania coal mines, while the women ran a small farm. Hart now lives outside Seattle, Washington.